THE KASHMIR HAND-BOOK- A GUIDE FOR VISITORS

THE KASHMIR HAND-BOOK- A GUIDE FOR VISITORS

JOHN INCE

GYAN

Published by

Gyan Publishing House
5, Ansari Road
Daryaganj, New Delhi-110002
Phone: 011-47034999, 9811692060
E-mail: books@gyanbooks.com

Distribution Network
gyanbooks.com
India, USA, Canada, UK, Australia

ISBN: 978-93-7414-127-4 (PB)

First Published, 1876

2nd Impression 2026

Printed at: Gyan Press, Delhi.

THE KASHMIR HAND-BOOK-A GUIDE FOR VISITORS
Author: JOHN INCE

THE

KASHMIR HAND-BOOK:

A

GUIDE FOR VISITORS.

WITH MAP AND ROUTES.

BY

JOHN INCE, M.D., M.R.C.S., L.S.A.L.,

SURGEON-MAJOR, BENGAL MEDICAL SERVICE,

SURGEON ON SPECIAL DUTY IN KASHMIR DURING THE SEASON OF 1864 & 1865.

THIRD EDITION, REVISED AND ENLARGED.

Calcutta:

WYMAN AND CO., PUBLISHERS, HARE STREET.

1876.

THE

KASHMIR HAND-BOOK:

A

GUIDE FOR VISITORS.

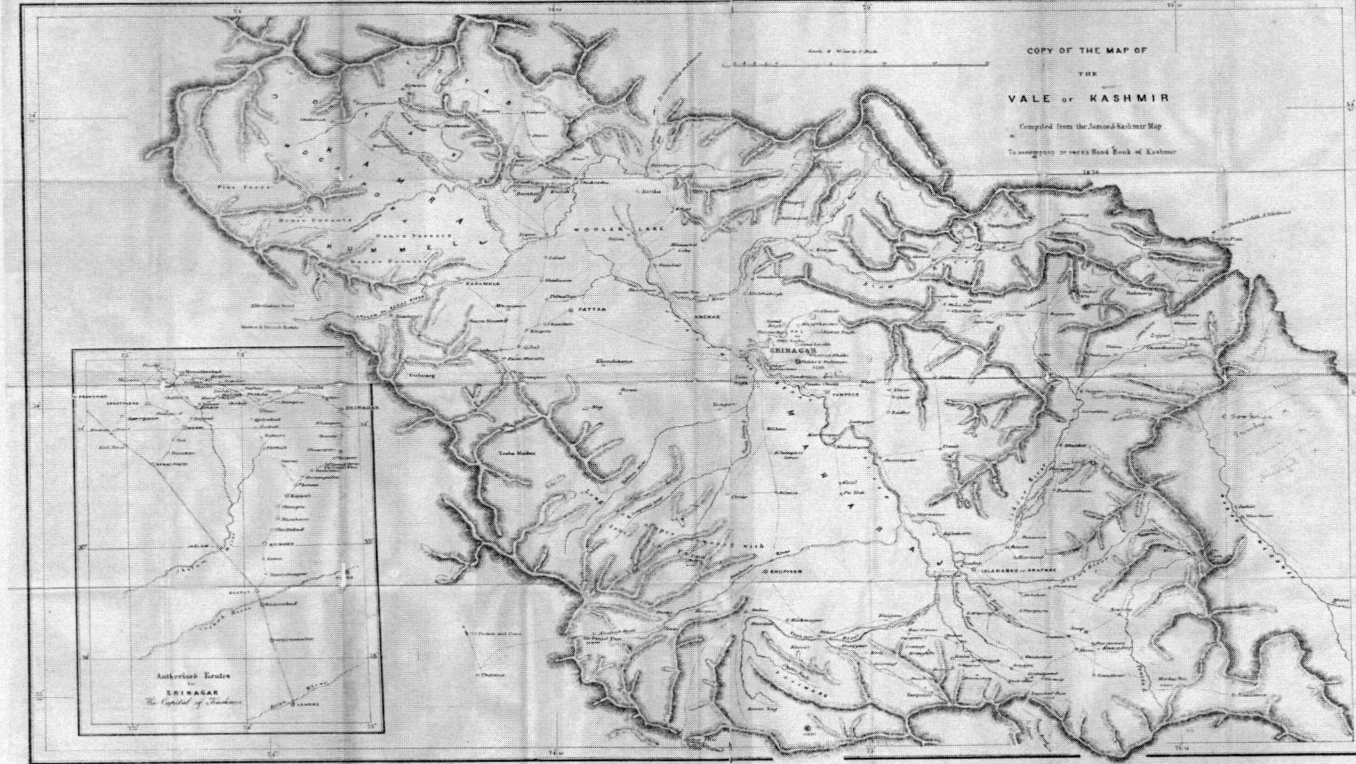
COPY OF THE MAP OF
THE
VALE OF KASHMIR
Compiled from the Jamoo & Kashmir Map
WOOLAR LAKE
PATTAN
SRINAGAR
SHUPIYAN
ISLAMABAD or ANATNAG
Authorised Routes
SRINAGAR

By the same Author,

MURREE AND ITS ENVIRONS,

WITH MAP AND KEY.

Sold for the benefit of the Murree Charitable Hospital. Honorary Agents: A. SCOTT & Co., Rawalpindi and Murree.

PRICE—TWO RUPEES, CASH.

CONTENTS.

APPENDIX.

PREFACE TO THE PRESENT EDITION.

ANOTHER Edition of this Hand-book having become exhausted, and in so short a time as to show an increasing demand for it, the Author has endeavoured by a complete revision to make the present one still more deserving of the confidence and approbation which its predecessors have enjoyed. A recent visit to the *Vale of Kashmir* has enabled him to make such corrections and additions as were needed by the changes of the past ten years. The progress during that time has been very marked, especially as regards the condition of the people and the country; the present arrangements for the comfort and convenience of Visitors too are now so complete and considerate as to merit their best acknowledgments to the Kashmir Government.

RAWALPINDI,
PANJAB, INDIA,
January 1876.

PREFACE TO THE SECOND EDITION.

THE object of this Hand-book, as stated in the previous edition—some time exhausted—is to provide the intending *Tourist in Kashmir* with a general description of that beautiful Province; to describe the four authorized *Routes to Srinagar*, its Capital; to conduct him to the various places and objects of interest in different parts of the country; and, at the same time, to offer such preliminary hints as may prove useful in ensuring his comfort and convenience during the tour.

His residence in Kashmir, as Medical Officer, during the seasons of 1864 and 1865, afforded the Author unusual opportunities for collecting materials for a Visitor's Guide; and in preparing it he is not only indebted for valuable information to the Assistant Secretary to the Punjab Government, the Secretary to the Asiatic Society of Bengal, and to numerous friends, whose notes were placed at his disposal, but he has also availed himself of the excellent works of *Vigne*, *Moorcroft*, *Hügel*, *Newal*, and others.

The plan of the work remains much the same; but the present edition has been entirely revised, and alterations and additions have been made with the view of rendering it as safe a guide as possible, and correct to the latest date. Many details as to measurements and other *minutiæ* have been omitted, whilst amongst other things the historical portions have been increased, and the routes to *Sonamarg* and the *Cave of Ambarnath* have been more fully given. A copy of the *Treaty on Trade with Eastern Turkestán*, and the *Postal Rules*, have been added to the *Appendix;* and, though last not least, a more complete map of the "Vale of Kashmír," with the routes to it has been expressly prepared for this edition.

Cordial acknowledgments are due for the assistance afforded by the *Rev. J. Long*, who last year visited the Province, and by *Kirpa Ram*, the Prime Minister, himself the author of a very learned Persian work upon this part of his Sovereign's dominions.

It would have been beyond the scope of this Hand-book to have described the adjoining valleys of *Gurais*, *Tilail*, *Dráwar*, and *Karnár*, or the neighbouring States of *Maru-Wardwan*, *Sooroo*, *Drás*, *Ladák*, *Astor*, *Baltistán*, *Chilás*, and *Khágán*; this is mainly a guide to the Valley of Kashmír, and in preparing it the Author has always borne in mind the interests of ladies and children, describing those places chiefly which are accessible to them. The *Sportsman*, however, will find a reliable note upon the game of Kashmir and the neighbouring regions in Appendix No 5; and the *Angler* is referred to the Index, where, under the head of Fishing, he will be guided to the places most famous for a successful cast. Those who are desirous of obtaining further information regarding the Province and those adjacent to it, may consult any or all the works given in the list which, for their assistance, is appended.

The Author, in conclusion, again requests that those visitors who have the leisure and literary ability—and there are many such—will have the goodness to forward notes of any changes or alterations they may observe in the course of their tour, to the Publishers, who are anxious to maintain the favorable character of this the only book of the kind as yet prepared regarding the "HAPPY VALLEY."

JOHN INCE, M.D.,
Civil Surgeon.

RAWALPINDI,
15*th October*, 1872.

LIST OF WORKS RELATING TO KASHMIR.

Bernier's Travels in India: A series of letters in French concerning his Journey to Kashmir in Aurungzib's Suite, 1670.

Forster's Letters: a Journey from Bengal to St. Petersburgh, 1783.

Moorcroft's Travels in 1820 in the Himalayan Provinces, Hindoostan, Punjáb, Ladák, and Kashmir, 1841.

Correspondence of Victor Jacquemont during his Travels in India, 1831.

Voyage dan L'Inde par V. Jacquemont. 4to. Tomes 2 and 3.

Cunningham's Ancient Geography of India, 1870.

Prinsep's Life of Runjit Singh.

Newal's Sketch of the Mohammedan History of Kashmir.—Journal Asiatic Society of Bengal, 1853-54.

Fryer's Histoire de Kasmeir: A Translation of the Rajtaringini.

Retter's Geography of Asia.

Researches and Missionary Labors by the Revd. Joseph Wolff, 1832.

Vigne's Travels in Kashmir, Ladák, Iskardó, &c., 1842.

Baron Hügel's Travels in Kashmir and Punjab, 1845.

Knight's Diary of a Pedestrian in Kashmir and Thibet, 1863.

Major Rennel's Memoirs of a Map of Hindustán, &c.

Schonberg's Travels in India and Kashmir.

Rajataringini. Translated by H. H. Wilson, Esq., as an "Essay on the Hindu History of Kashmir," in the Asiatic Researches or *Transactions of the Society*, Vol. XV., 1825.

Gulzar Kashmir. By Diwan Kirpa Ram, 1871.

Brinkman's Rifle in Kashmir.

Across the Karakorum. By an Officer.

Kashmiri Vocabulary and Notes. By Dr. W. J. Elmslie, Medical Missionary of the C. M. S.

Illustrations of Ancient Buildings in Kashmir. By Lieutenant Henry Hardy Cole, R. E.

Large Game Shooting in Thibet and the North-West. By A. A. A. Kinloch, Major, Rifle Brigade, 1869.

Letters from India and Kashmir, written in 1870. Published in 1874, by George Bell & Sons, London.

The Jummoo and Kashmir Territories. By Frederick Drew, F. R. G. S. & F. G. S., London: Stanford, 1875.

Kashmir and Yarkand. By H. W. Bellew, C. S. I., Bengal Medical Service; London, 1875.

Goheri Alem Tohfet us, Shahi of Badia-ud-din, in the time of the last Shah Alem.

Ayin-Akberi, The. By Abul Fazel.

A History by an unknown Persian Author, containing a long list of Princes and Legends.

A History of the Mohammedan Kingdoms of India. By Mohammed Kasim Ferishta.

The History of Kashmir. By Múllah Hussun Kári.

The History of Kashmir. By Hyder Malik Shad-Waria.

Tarikh-i-Kashmir. By Naráyn Kúl, in the reign of Mohammed Shah.

Wakiat-i-Kashmir. By Mohammed Azim, in the year 1140 H., in the reign of Mohammed Shah.

Nawádir-ul-Akbar. By Mohammed Rafia-ud-din, 1133 Hijra.

Toozek Jehangeery; or, Memoirs of Jehangir, in *Asiatic Misc.*, Vol. II.

Núr Númeh. By Shaikh Nur-ud-deen, in the Kashmirian language; translated into Persian by Múlvi Ahmet, Almeh, in the reign of Zinal-ab-u-din.

History of Kashmir under the Afghans; written in Persian by Múlvi Khair-ud-din.

Hagus de Rebus Japonicis, Indicis, &c., 1609.

Les Lettres Edifiantes de quelques Missionaires de la Compagnie de Jesus.

KASHMIR HAND-BOOK.

CHAPTER I.

THE PROVINCE OF KASHMIR.

Geographical Situation—Ancient Division—The Vale of Kashmir—Its Great Celebrity—Passes— Rivers— Bridges—Boats—Lakes Springs—Kareewahs—Physical History—Climate—Natural Productions—Animals—Vegetation—Minerals— Inhabitants — Physique and Moràle—Language— Dress—Food—Arts and Manufactures—Government—Laws—Administrative Divisions—Revenue—Trade and Commerce—Military Forces—The History of Kashmir—Ancient Rulers—Mogul Emperors—Pathán Rulers—Sikhs—The Present Sovereign—Religion—Antiquities—Literature.

Geographical situation.

1. Kashmir* is a mountainous country, embedded in that portion of the great Himalayas which skirts the north-western border of Hindústán. It is bounded North by *Astor*, *Iskardo*, and other districts of *Little Tibet*; East, by *Drás*, *Sooroo*, *Zanskar*, and *Ladák*; South, by *Poonch*, *Naoshera*, *Kishtawár*, *Badrawár*, and *Jamoo*, and the British districts of *Jhelam*, *Goojrát*, and *Siálkote*; and West, by *Khághán*, and the British districts

* The origin of the word *Kashmir* has been the subject of much speculation; according to Professor *H. H. Wilson*, however, it is derived from *Kashuf*, the Mohamedan name of *Kusyapa*, one of the divine sages of Hindú history, and the *deo* or gin employed by *Solomon* according to tradition, to drain the Valley. It is variously spelt as *Cashmere Cashmeer: Cashmire:* the letter *K* is often substituted for the initial C.

of *Hazára* and *Ráwalpindi*. Its area is about 25,000 square miles, and its present population is estimated at about 425,000 souls. It forms a portion of the dominions of the Maharajah of *Jamoo*, a feudatory of the British Government, and son of the late *Golab Singh*, to whom it was transferred in March, 1846.*

Ancient divisions.

2. In ancient times the province was divided into two portions—*Simit Máharáj* and *Simit Kamráj*. The former comprised all that part of it lying to the southward of a line drawn through the *Woolar Lake* from *Bandipore* along the Jhelam to *Báramoola;* and the latter all to the north of the same line. These were again divided into thirty-six *pergannahs* or *hundreds*, the names of which are marked in the *Jamoo and Kashmir map*, and are given below:—

List of the Pergannahs of Kashmir.

No.	Name.	Chief Town.
1	Banihál	
2	Sháhabád	Sháhabád.
3	Bringh	Ságám.
4	Kotihár	
5	Diosir	Koolgàm.
6	Arwin	Arwin.
7	Batoo	Shupiyan.

* See Appendix No. 1.

List of the Pergannahs of Kashmir—(Continued.)

No.	Name.	Chief Town.
8	Sapar Saman	
9	Zainapoor	
10	Shookroor	
11	Showra	
12	Nágám	Chrár,
13	Yech	Yechgám.
14	Doonsoo	
15	Birwa	Birwa.
16	Manchahámа	
17	Bangil	
18	Salimosa Paieen ...	Súmbal
19	Kroohin	
20	Kaur	
21	Dachin	
22	Hammel	
23	Móchipora	
24	Zainagir	Sopoor.
25	Ootar	
26	Loláb	Lálpoor.
27	Quihámа	Bandipoora.
28	Lár	Noonur.
29	Phak	Shálimár.
30	Vihi	Pámpoor.
31	Woolar	Traál.
32	Selimoza Bála	Bijbehára.
33	Dachinpára	Pálgám.
34	Kaurpára	Eishmakám.
35	Mártand	Báwan.
36	Anatnág	Islámabád.

3. Kashmir consists chiefly of one large and beautiful valley, which is entirely surrounded by lofty snow-clad moun-

Vale of Kashmir.

tains, traversed by the river *Jhelam*, and fringed, so to speak, by numerous glens and minor valleys, which open into it on every side. The main valley is the far-famed VALE OF KASHMIR.

> Who has not heard of the Vale of Cashmere,
> With its roses the brightest that earth ever gave;
> Its temples, and grottos, and fountains as clear
> As the love-lighted eyes that hang over their wave?
>
> MOORE'S "*Làlla Rookh.*"

It is irregularly oblong in shape, lying north-west and south-east; it is about 100 miles in length, with an average of 25 miles in width; its average height is about 5,200 feet above the level of the sea, and its area about 4,500 square miles. The surrounding mountains vary in height from 8,000 to 15,000 feet: those on the southern side are a portion of the *Pir Panjál*—a range extending over 400 miles—and their formation is chiefly *basaltic* and *shale;* their sides are covered with dense forests, and their summits usually crowned with snow: those on the northern side are still higher, mostly of mountain limestone, generally bare and rugged, and their loftier peaks, as *Haramook* and others, are also covered with perpetual snow. The chief *minor valleys* opening into it are the *Loláb* and the *Sind* on the north, the *Liddar* on the north-east, the *Nowboog* on the east, and several

Minor valleys.

smaller ones on its southern side. On the tops of many of the surrounding hills there are beautiful grassy valleys, or mountain meadows, called *margs:* the principal are *Gulmarg, Sonamarg, Zojimarg,* and *Rubmarg,* and there are several smaller ones in the vicinity of the two latter. They vary greatly in extent, but are all covered with rich pasturage, many kinds of English flowers, and during the summer months they are crowded with immense herds of goats, sheep, ponies, and cattle, which depasture there under the care of their *chopáns, gulabáns, goojroos,* and other herdsmen, who live in log huts of their own construction.

Margs.

4. The Valley of Kashmir has been compared to *a gem* in the everlasting Himalayas as its casket, and its charming scenery, delicious climate, fertile soil, and choice productions have rendered it celebrated from the earliest times and throughout the world. It is an *oasis* in the midst of rocks, snow, and glaciers, and is regarded as a *Holy Land* alike by Hindús and Mohamedans. The former consider it to have been the first paradise in the *Máha Yúg,* and the Moslems believe the same. Its noble ruins and its various ancient coins proclaim alike its former greatness and antiquity. It was the favorite summer retreat of the *Mogul Emperors,* who built the

Its great celebrity.

costly palaces and planned those numerous pleasure gardens, which even yet so much adorn it. Until within about the last thirty years it had been visited by very few Europeans,* but in consequence of its having been entirely thrown open, there has lately been an annually increasing number of visitors, not only from all parts of India, but from Europe and even from America, which testifies to its great attractions, and justifies the statement of the historian *Elphinstone,* that it "still maintains its celebrity as the most delicious spot in Asia or in the world."

Passes leading into it.

5. The passes leading into the valley are numerous. *Abú Fazl* says there are 26, but an active mountaineer could enter it in many other places than by the regular passes. There is not one of them fit for wheeled carriages, but a road might, though at considerable expense, be constructed along the banks of the Jhelam, from *Mozufferabad* to *Báramoola.* The following are the names of the principal passes :—

* *Xavier,* a Spanish Jesuit, along with *Goez,* attended *Akbar* to Kashmir about 1594, as *Bernier,* a French physician, did *Aurangzib* in 1665,—as his doctor. The Jesuit missionary *Desideri* spent the winter of 1714 there. *Forster,* a Madras civilian, also spent some time there about 1786, and thence proceeded over the Kashmir mountains to St. Petersburgh *via* Central Asia. *Moorcroft,* accompanied by *Trebeck* and *Guthrie* visited it in 1823; *Jacquemont,* in 1831; *Wolff,* in 1832; and *Baron Hugel, Vigne,* and *Dr. Henderson* met together at *Srinagar* on the 18th November. 1835.

List of the principal Passes into the Kashmir Valley.

Situation.	Name.	Height.	From whence.
South	Pir Panjál ...	11,400	Bhimbar and Rájáorí.
"	Báramoola ...	?	Marri Poonch Abbotabad.
"	Ferózepore ...	?	Poonch and Rájáorí.
"	Banihál ...	9,200	Jamoo.
East	Marbal ...	11,570	Kishtawár and Chamba.
"	Margan ...	11,600	Maroo Wardwan and Sooroo.
North	Zojilá or Drás ...	11,300	Dras and Ladák.
"	Rájdiangan ...	11,800	Gurais, Tilail, Little Tibet.
West	Tootmári Galli ...	?	Karnár.
"	Naschau Galli ...	?	Karnár.
"	Patti Khair ...	?	Dráwar.

Rivers.

The Jhelam.

6. The principal rivers are the *Jhelam*, *Veshau*, *Liddar*, *Sind*, and *Pohra*. The *Jhelam*—the *Hydaspes* of the Greeks, the *Vetastha* of the Hindús, and the *Vehat* of the Mohamedans—is the principal one, and it nearly intersects the whole length of the valley. It commences about a mile to the south-east of *Kanbal*, near *Islámabád*, where it is formed by the junction of three streams—the *Arpat*, the *Bringh*, and the *Sandrahán*—which rise chiefly from numerous springs at the eastern end of the valley. From *Kanbal* to *Báramoola*—a distance of about 60 miles—it is broad and smooth, navigable nearly all the year round, and moves at the rate

of about 1½ to 3 miles an hour, according to its height. For the most part it flows nearer the north-eastern than the south-western side of the valley, but after passing through the *Woolar Lake* it turns more southward, and leaves it through the gorge immediately below *Bára-moola.* Its banks are generally level and canal-like, and its channel is usually sufficient for carrying off the rain, as well as the melting snow from the surrounding mountains. In July and August it rises about 12 feet above its usual level, and now and then it overflows its banks, the dams and sluices give way, the whole country becomes flooded, and resembles an extensive lake, the people are obliged to take to their boats, and notwithstanding the assistance and liberality of the *Maharajah,* their distress and loss are sometimes very great. Two such floods occurred in each of the years 1865 and 1871, and they will be long remembered by those visitors who were then at Srinagar, and suffered the inconveniences produced by them.

Its tributaries.

7. The principal tributaries which join its right bank are the *Liddar*, by two branches just below *Kanbal*, the *Sind* at *Shadipoor*, and the *Pohra* at *Dabgao*, a little below *Sopoor*; those which join its left bank are the *Veshau* near *Marháma*, the *Ramchu* at *Karkarpoor*, and the *Dúdhgan-*

ga immediately below *Srinagar*. It also receives the waters of the following lakes, viz. :—The *Dal* and *Anchar* near Srinagar, and the *Mánasbal* and *Woolar* below Súmbal.

Bridges.

8. In its course through the valley it is crossed by 13 bridges, which are all made with trunks of the *deodar* or Himalayan cedar, and in the following manner :—A triangular space in the bed of the river is enclosed, with its apex stream-wards, by long stakes well driven down and covered on the outside with planks to the height of about 8 feet; this space is then filled in with large and heavy stones, and forms the foundation of the pier. This consists of alternate layers of deodar trunks placed about a foot apart, and fastened at both ends to the subjacent ones by strong wooden pegs; each succeeding layer being broader than the preceding one and laid at right angles to it, so that the shape of the piers is that of a truncated and inverted cone. The piers are united by other and longer trunks laid about two feet apart, and across them planks or slender poles are placed to complete the platform. In some cases this is covered with a layer of earth or dry grass, and provided with a railing on each side to protect passengers, but in most cases there is neither. The following is a list of the bridges :—

List of Bridges across the Jhelam in the Kashmir Valley.

No.		NAME.	Length.	Breadth.	Number of piers.	Average depth of water.
			Yards.	Feet.		Feet.
1		Kanbal	66	12	1	4½
2		Bijbehára	100	17	3	6
3		Pámpur	132	14	4	6½
4	City of Srinagar.	Ameeri Kadal ...	134	20	5	16
5	City of Srinagar.	Habba Kadal ...	97	24	3	16
6	City of Srinagar.	Futteh Kadal ...	88	17	3	16
7	City of Srinagar.	Zaina Kadal ...	96	24	3	16
8	City of Srinagar.	Alli Kadal ...	82	17	3	16
9	City of Srinagar.	Naya Kadal ...	75	18	3	16
10	City of Srinagar.	Saffa Kadal ...	110	19	4	16
11		Súmbul	112	16	4	15
12		Sópur	214	16	3	28
13		Báramúla	146	16	6	24

River boats.

9. The boats used upon the Kashmir rivers are of four principal kinds, viz.: the *doongah*, the *shikára*, the *varh*, and the *bahatz*. Only the two first, however, are used by visitors, the others being large barge-like vessels employed in transporting grain, wood, and other produce to different parts of the valley. In the time of *Akbar* the number of registered boats exceeded, it is said, 8,900. The use of sails is almost unknown, and as yet only one steamer has been launched upon the waters of Kashmir,

that being the gift of H. E. the Viceroy of India to H. H. the Maharajah.

The doongah.

10. The doongah—the ordinary excursion boat of Kashmir—is a long, flat-bottomed craft, usually about 56 feet in length, $5\frac{3}{4}$ feet in width, and $1\frac{3}{4}$ feet in depth. It is covered for more than half its length by an awning of matting supported upon a light wooden roof about $5\frac{1}{2}$ feet high, to the sides of which separate pieces are attached, to be let down at pleasure, either to secure privacy or shelter from sun or rain. The crew usually consists of four persons, men and women, who with their families live all the year round in the hinder part of the boat. Down-stream it is propelled by short and heart-shaped paddles, while up-stream it is drawn along the bank by a long towing line. The rate of hire for a boat and crew of four persons is 18 British rupees a month, or so much for each journey. Each boat is capable of containing a bed, a table, a chair, and other small articles of furniture, including kitchen utensils, and also the servants: for the latter, however, it is more agreeable to engage a separate one.

The shikára.

11. The shikára or punt, is of the same shape as the *doongah*, but smaller, being usually only about 36 feet long, $3\frac{1}{2}$ feet wide, and 1 foot deep. This is chiefly used as a gig,

when moving about in and near Srinagar. The crew generally consists of six men, who propel the boat by small and heart-shaped paddles: the rate of hire is the same as that for the *doongah.* If, however, they are taken beyond the vicinity of the city, the boatmen are entitled, unless their *doongah* is also engaged, to an extra anna a day each.

12. There are numerous lakes about Kashmir, both in the valley itself and on the mountains surrounding it. Of the former, the principal are the *Dal* or City lake—the most famous of all and inseparably associated with the love-quarrel of *Jehángir* and his fair *Núr Mehal**—situated on the north-eastern side of Srinagar, and connected with the Jhelam by the *Sunt-i-kul*, or apple tree, canal, which joins it opposite the Palace; the *Mánasbal* —the smallest but most beautiful—situated near the right bank of the Jhelam, which it joins by a canal just below Súmbal; and the *Woolar*, by far the largest of all, and situated in the western portion of the valley. Of the *mountain lakes* the following are the chief:—The *Konsa Nág,* situated on the top of the Panjál, above the village of Sedau; the *Sheesha Nág*, situated beyond the head of the Liddar Valley, and on the path to the cave of Ambernáth; and *Gangabal*, situated on the top

Lakes.

* See "The Light of the Haram," in MOORE's "*Lalla Rookh.*"

of the Haramúk, which overlooks the Woolar and the valley of the Sind. There are also other minor ones—as the *Mar Sar*, *Tar Sar*, *Sona Sar*, *Chanda Sar*, and *Hokar Sar*, near the Jojimarg; the *Nila Nág* and *Bagh Sar*, a little to the south of the Tosha Maidan; and *Deo Sar*, a little north of Chogal, in Kamráj.

Springs.

13. The springs of Kashmir are innumerable, issuing from the sides and feet of the mountains in all directions, as well as from several places in the centre of the valley itself. The finest are in its eastern portion, and they form the principal sources of the Jhelam; amongst them are the *Anat Nág*, *Báwan*, *Atchibal*, *Vernág*, *Kookar Nág*, and the *Vateritter*. There are also several *mineral* springs, of which the Weean near Pampoor, and the *Salik* and *Malick Nágs* at Islamabad, are the chief; they contain *iron* and *sulphuretted hydrogen*, and their medicinal virtues, especially those of the *Weean*, are doubtless very great. This famous spring is slightly warm, as is also the case with several others in different parts of the province.

Kareewahs.

14. Along the edges of the main valley, especially its southern, there are several elevated table-lands called *kareewahs*, which are alluvial plains varying in height from 100 to 200 feet, and in length from 2 to 5 miles. The princi-

pal are those of *Pámpoor* and *Islámabád* on the northern, and *Zynapoor*, *Nonágar*, *Khánpoor*, and *Damúdar* on the southern side. They are separated from each other by wide and deep ravines cut by the streams from the adjoining mountains. They form one of the most interesting and striking topographical features of the valley, and, with the numerous masses of shingle found in various parts of it,—as those near *Ramoo*, those on the southern face of the hill of Islamabad, those on the mountain side along the road between this town and *Báwan*, those near the *Vateritter spring*, a little west of Vernág, and especially those near *Malshabágh*, on the road from Srinagar to Gánderbal,—tend to confirm the truth of the local legend that in bygone ages it was one vast mountain lake.

Physical history of the valley.

15. · With reference to this subject and the formation of the *kareewahs* just described, General A. Cunningham writes as follows* :—"The rocky cliffs below Tattamoola, and about 16 miles below Baramoola, rise almost perpendicularly from the river (Jhelam) to a height of 300 and 400 feet, and in some places that I noticed, the bare steep cliffs were not less than 800 feet above the stream. As the height of the *Behut* (Jhelam) near Tattamoola is about 5,000 feet above the sea, the whole of Kashmir must

* *Vide Cunningham's* "LADAK," p. 114.

have been submerged by the waters of the river before the wearing down of these cliffs. The level of the Kashmirian lake would have been about 5,800 feet above the sea, and from 50 to 100 feet above the *kareewahs* or isolated alluvial flats now remaining in Kashmir......... The high level land of Mártand was probably not submerged, but the horizontal beach-marks are still quite distinct on the limestone cliffs above the Cave of Bhaumájo* and the Holy Sping of Báwun. Above Ramoo-ke-serai, on the Shupiyan river, the kareewah forms a bank about 100 feet in height, in horizontal strata of different kinds. The uppermost 20 feet are composed of stiff alluvial soil; the next 20 feet, of rolled stones and loose earth; and the lowermost 60, of indurated blue clay. The last must have been deposited by the lake in its state of quiescence; but the middle stratum could only have been formed by the first grand rush of waters, on some sudden burst of the rocky barrier below *Tattamooia*, and the uppermost would have been deposited by the subsiding waters as they reached the newly-formed level. Then, as the rocky bed was gradually worn down, the different streams worked new channels for themselves in the former bed of the lake, until the present *kareewahs* of Nonagar, Pampur, and Kánikpur (Khánpur), were left, first as islands in the decreasing lake, and eventually

* *Vide* Chapter IV.

as long, flat-topped hills in the midst of the open plain, just as we now see them."

16. Kashmir, from its greater elevation, is much cooler than the plains of India. The climate of the lower portions of the valley resembles that of the south of Europe, while that of the surrounding mountains is more like that of Norway and Lapland. As a health-resort the province has no rival anywhere near to Hindústàn; its climate is admirably adapted to the European constitution, and, in consequence of the varied range of temperature, and the facility of moving about, the visitor is enabled with ease to select those spots which are most congenial to him. Indeed, to those requiring a change from the plains of India on account of ill-health, a few months' residence in Kashmir will be found almost as beneficial as a trip to Europe. In certain disordered functions of the female system its bracing effects are *specially* remarkable, and several instances are known in which the long-deferred hopes of maternity have been fully realized by a few months' sojourn in the *Happy Valley*. The *hottest months* are July and August, during which the temperature in the shade, at noon, varies from 85° to 90°, and occasionally to 95° at Srinagar, which is probably the hottest place in the valley; the air is then often close and oppressive, especially for a

Climate.

day or two before a fall of rain, which is usually accompanied by thunder and lightning. The *coldest months* are December and January, during which the average morning temperature at Srinagar is a little below the freezing point, and the lakes and ponds, as well as the Jhelam itself, occasionally, are frozen over. The *seasons* are all pretty well marked in the valley; but the surrounding mountains are subject to periodical rains, which occur about the same time as in Hindústán. The total annual *fall of rain* and snow upon the latter must be very great; but in the valley the quantity is by no means so. Frequent and sudden storms of rain and hail, however, occur about the end of March and beginning of April, and showers are numerous in May; in June and September heavy falls of rain are common, and occasional showers occur in July and August. The first *fall of snow* upon the mountains usually occurs about the beginning of October, but it is slight and soon melts; the heavy fall begins, both on the mountains and in the plains, about the middle of December, and then remains until the end of April, after which it disappears, except from the crests and peaks of the higher mountains and the deep and secluded gorges on their northern sides. *Earthquakes* are pretty frequent during the summer months, and hence, it is said, the reason for building the houses of wood; the shocks, although usually slight, are occasionally very severe and destructive,—as in 1552, again about 1680, and on 26th June 1828, on which latter occasion Vigne states that about 1,200 houses were shaken down and about 1,000 persons killed.

Natural productions.

The natural productions of Kashmir are very numerous; the *animals* resemble those found in other portions of the Himalayas. Of the *domestic species*, the horse, cow, and ox are very small; the first are of two kinds—*ghoonts* and *yaboos*—and are more numerous in *Kamraj* than in *Maharaj*, though in the latter, especially the pergannas of *Dachinpara*, *Shahabad*, *Brengh*, and *Kotihar*, they are stronger and better bred. Their price varies from 10 to 100 rupees. exclusive of a Government tax of 2½ annas per rupee. *Yarkand ponies*—the strongest in Asia—may occasionally be purchased from the merchants passing through Kashmir to the Panjab. To the Hindùs the *cow* is a very sacred animal, and the greatest caution is desirable to avoid offending this religious prejudice. The animals cannot be purchased in Kashmir, but, when necessary for sick children or other urgent purposes, they can be borrowed. Visitors bringing their own cows into the valley, are invited, on leaving, to make them over on purchase to the officials there, in order that they may be

Animals.

saved the fatigues and hardships of another mountain journey. *Sheep* are of good size and their flesh well-flavored; their prices vary from 1 to 5 rupees each. The barn door *fowl* and *duck* are very common, and *water fowl* and *fish* of various kinds are equally abundant. *Flies, mosquitoes, sand flies,* and many other species of insects are numerous and very troublesome, particularly in moist places, and in the months of August and September. *Bees* are kept by most cottagers in circular holes in the walls of their huts, especially by those living in the eastern portion of the valley: the honey is excellent. The *silkworm* is bred extensively there also, and its culture has of late years been very warmly undertaken by the Government. The *heron* is carefully preserved for its feathers, the use of which, as plumes for the turban, is restricted to those of the highest rank. Of the other wild animals, the *monkey, fox, jackal, bear,* and *leopard,* are most common; but the *ibex, márkhor, bara singh,* and many other kinds of game abound in the neighbouring mountains.

Vegetation.

18. The soil of the valley is a very rich and fertile alluvium, which, aided by a moist atmosphere and a genial temperature, usually yields luxuriant crops of cereals and other articles of food, which are consequently very cheap.

Those portions which are uncultivated are also covered with wild fruit and other trees, as the *walnut, mulberry, peach, cherry, apricot, pomegranate, hazel-nut, apple, quince, pear,* the *plane,** *poplar, willow,* and many others. The climate is too cold for *mangoes, oranges,* and *melons;* but nearly all the English garden vegetables grow in great perfection. The *grapes* are very fine; there are some eighteen kinds of them, and excellent wine may be produced. The manufacture of *perry* and *cider* was tried by the Government a few years since, but the results were not successful, owing most likely to faulty management. The *misletoe* grows there. *Cotton* is produced, but only in small quantity: the clothing material is chiefly wool. *Saffron* is extensively cultivated about Pampoor. Numerous *medicinal plants* are found growing wild, as *wormwood (tetwin), chiretta, aloes, rhubarb, colocynth, Indian hemp,* and others. *Prungus*—a species of grass found at elevations of about 6,000 to 7,000 feet—is collected and used as fodder for cattle in the winter, and its root is used as a remedy for foot-rot in sheep. The inner bark of the plane tree somewhat resembles *cork,* and a resin like *gutta-percha* is extracted from a plant called *dhup:* the utility of these

* The *plane* or *chenar* tree is not indigenous, but was introduced by the Governor, *Alli Mardàn Khan,* who ruled there under the Moguls from 1642 to 1657. As *Long* observes, it has remained when mosques and marble palaces have passed away.

two products is not yet fully determined. The sides of the surrounding mountains are also covered with herbage and rich grass, and their northern sides are clothed with dense forests of pine, deodar, and other trees. But, notwithstanding the usual fertility of the soil, famines occur occasionally, and the consequences to the inhabitants, chiefly from the badness of the roads and the difficulty of transport, are sometimes very terrible, especially as they are usually followed by an outbreak of cholera or some other epidemic.

Minerals.

19. The mineral resources of Kashmir are as yet probably but little known. *Iron* is worked at Arwan, near Sopoor; at Shar, near Pampoor; and at Soap, near Islamabad. *Lead*, *sulphur*, and *copper* probably exist in various parts. *Lignite* has been discovered, and *silver* and even *gold* may yet be found. There is no *table salt*, and the supply of this essential condiment is all obtained from the Panjab plains.

Inhabitants.

20. The inhabitants of Kashmir are chiefly *Mohamedans*,* and of the *Súni* sect; there are a few *Hindús*—about one-

* The bitterness of religious feeling betwen the Sùnees and the Shiahs, the rival sects of Mohamedans—is extreme, and occasionally breaks out very fiercely, ending in bloody affrays, loss of life, and extensive demolition of property in that quarter of the city of Srinagar in which the Shiahs, who are comparatively few in number, reside. One of these riots occurred during 1874, and the assistance of the troops became necessary to suppress it, as it continued for some days.

seventh of the whole population—and they reside for the most part at Srinagar, and the other large towns. The Mohamedans have many sacred shrines or *zearuts* in various parts of the valley, but the principal ones are *Sháh Núrúdín*, at *Chrár; Hazratbal,* on the *Dal or City Lake;* and that of *Bába Pyúmdín Rishi*, at Bába Marishi. The tribes or families are numerous, but the *Cháks* are the most important; they were the old warrior class, and about 1536, having assumed regal power, they bravely defended their country against the *Moguls, Tartars, Kashgarris, Turks*, and other enemies. In later times, however, they degenerated into bands of brigands, which infested some of the most frequented roads in Kashmir; but about the beginning of this century they were finally hunted down to their mountain homes, and rigorously punished by the Sikh Governor, *Kirpa Rám.* They are now represented chiefly by the *gúlúwans* or horse-keepers, who tend their herds upon the margs or mountain downs. The *Rishis* were another important class; they were holy men, resembling the monks of Europe and the *fakirs* of India; some of them were held in great reverence, were canonised, and have had shrines erected to their memory, called *zearust*, or places of visitation, which are very famous, and annually resorted to by thousands of pilgrims. The *Hindús*, though few in number, are now the favored class,

Hindús.

the present reigning dynasty being *Dogras*, a sect of the Hindús. They also have some very sacred places, a few indeed being famed throughout India; the principal ones are the *Cave of Ambernath,* the lakes of *Gangabal* and *Sheesha Nág*, and the springs of *Anat Nág* and *Bawan.* They are also divided into several families, but the *Pundits*—learned Brahmins, teachers and interpreters of the *Shástras* and other sacred writings—are the chief. *Long* says of these, that they are the only living representatives of the past in Kashmir, and that their influence ought to be utilized to a greater extent than it is, because they have a great name for their learning, and in certain branches some of them still hold a high position. They are in general more robust and manly-looking than those of Bengal, retaining more of the primitive *Aryan* type of feature; they wear the beard, take snuff, but do not smoke, and, like all Kasmiris, are dirty and very rarely bathe. They share with other *pundits* throughout India contempt for the vernaculars, and therefore despise the Kashmir language; but they differ from most of them in writing in the Persian character, not even knowing the *Devanágri.* During the long period of Moslem rule they and Sanskrit literature were at a discount, and hence not only is their number limited, but their attainments in the latter are in general not profound. Having no regular colleges to foster their ancient literature, the range of their studies was restricted; but now a brighter day is dawning upon them,—the *Maharajah of Kashmir*, emulating the zeal of the rajahs and other influential natives throughout India in the cause of the *oriental classics*, has lately granted a *lac* of rupees *per annum* for the maintenance of two colleges—one at Jamoo, the other at Srinagar—and the *pundits* are now settled in comfortable quarters, mostly along the banks of the Jhelam.

Physique and *moràle.*

21. The people of Kashmir are physically a fine race, the men being tall, strong, and stoutly built; the complexion is usually olive, but sometimes—especially amongst the Hindús—fair and ruddy; the features are regular and well-shaped,—those of the Mahomedans, however having a decidedly Jewish caste, and in this resembling the *Pathans*. They are lively and intelligent, full of fun, and fond of amusement; the men and boys whistle and also sing, being loudly assisted in the latter by the women, the beauty of whom has been long and much extolled. The men are, now at least, by no means brave; and, upon the whole, the character of the Kashmiri is not an elevated one. Proverbs say of them: "Many fowls in a house will defile it: many Kashmiris in a country will spoil it." "If you meet

a snake, do not put it to death; but do not spare a Kashmiri." "Do not admit a Kashmiri to your friendship, or you will hang a hatchet over your door-way." Moorcroft* thus describes him:—"Selfish, superstitious, ignorant, supple, intriguing, dishonest, and false, he has great ingenuity as a mechanic, and a decided genius for manufactures and commerce; but his transactions are always conducted in a fraudulent spirit, equalled only by the effrontery with which he faces detection,"—not a flattering character certainly, and by no means universally true.

Language.

22. Their language is peculiar, and at first quite unintelligible to the visitor, from its being so unlike those he is accustomed to in the plains of India. It is a *prakrit* of the Sanskrit, as Italian is of the Latin. Vigne states that out of 100 words 40 will be *Persian*, 25 *Sanskrit*, 15 *Hindústani*, 10 *Arabic*, and the remainder *Tibetan*, or of other adjacent countries.

Dress.

23. On the conquest of Kashmir by the Mogul Emperor *Akbar*, about 1588, the ancient dress of the people was changed, and the present costumes imposed upon them. That of the men consists of a pair of very loose drawers, a long and loose shirt resembling the *smock frock* of our

* Moorcroft's "Travels in Kashmir, &c.," Vol. II., p. 128.

English labourers, and a *pagri* or turbun,—all of white colour. That of the women is a long shirt, with loose sleeves like the men, of red, blue, green, or white color; a skull cap surrounded with a fillet of red cloth; and a white *chaddar* or large veil, thrown gracefully over the head and shoulders, more as a protection from the sun than for concealment of the features, which latter custom is confined only to women of the highest class. The *Hindú* women also wear a white rolled cloth loosely bound round the waist, and many of them are profusely ornamented with elegant earrings, nose rings, anklets, and bracelets, especially the *punditánis*—the wives of the *pundits*—who are the fairest and most beautiful in the valley, prettier even than the boat women. Their mode of hair-dressing is peculiar; it is drawn to the back of the head and finely braided; the braids are then gathered together, and, being mixed with coarse woollen thread, are worked into a very long plait terminated by a thick tassel, which reaches almost down to the ankles: it is highly suggestive of the *Chinese pigtail*, but it is far more graceful. The summer clothes are usually made of cotton, but those for winter wear are of a thick woollen material. In the cold weather every Kashmiri, male and female, carries a *kángri*, which is a small earthen basin, somewhat like the charcoal-burner of Italy, about six inches in diameter, enclosed in a neat basket of wicker-work, and filled with live charcoal; some of them are exceedingly pretty, being tastefully ornamented with rings and painted in brilliant colors. They are applied next the skin to give warmth to the front of the body, and burns from them are very common—few grown-up persons, indeed, being free from a scar or two.

Food.

24. Nature is in general very bountiful in Kashmir, both on land and water, and food for the natives is, therefore, usually as cheap as it is abundant. Their average income may be estimated at about two British rupees a month, and this seems amply sufficient to provide them with food, clothing, and habitation, to preserve them in robust health, and, in short, to meet all their ordinary requirements. The staple article of food is *rice*, but *wheat*, *barley*, *maize*, and several other grains are cultivated. Vegetables, as *cabbages*, *turnips*, *kadoos*, *cucumbers*, *lettuces*, and many other varieties are also very abundant, and are extensively eaten. The leaves of the *dandelion*, *plantain*, and several other plants are made into soup. The stem of the *lotus*, when boiled and flavoured, is also eaten; it is called *nadrú*, is of a pale straw color, cylindrical, about 10 inches long and 1½ inch in diameter, and is considered highly nutritious. The water-nut or *singhára*, ground to flour and made into bread, forms the

principal article of diet of those who live on the margin of the great lakes. The flesh of sheep and goats is eaten by Mohammedans, and the Dogras relish pork—that is, of the wild boar—as much as Christians. *Beef* is, of course, unprocurable, the killing of kine being regarded by Hindùs as sacrilege—a crime worthy of death, which penalty until lately was always inflicted, and even now the punishment is a very severe one.

Arts and manufactures.

25. The Kashmiris are celebrated for their *weaving*, *embroidery*, *engraving*, and working in metals. The *shawls* are of world-wide reputation, and the woollen cloth of which they are made, and which is called *pushmína*, consists of the short or under-coat—the fleece or *pushm*—of the shawl-goat, immense herds of which are reared upon the mountains of Western Tibet. The manufacture is under Government control ; a duty is imposed upon every pair made, and the genuineness of the materials used, is secured by the infliction of heavy penalties in the case of adulteration : hence their superior value in the European markets. The *woven* ones are the most durable, and by far the most expensive, although the *hand-made* ones are at first sight the more striking. Besides shawls, many other articles of clothing, both of European and Native patterns, are made, such as *neckties*, *tippets*, *mantles*, *pagries*, *kam-*

marbands, &c. *Pattoo* is a coarser kind of cloth than *pushmina;* it is made in pieces of various patterns, is cheap, and is very suitable for ladies and children's dresses, as well as gentleman's suits. The *leather,* owing to the mode of tanning, is of excellent quality; and first-rate *saddlery, trunks, boots, shoes, chaplees,* and other useful articles may be easily and cheaply purchased. The *papier-maché* is much admired. The *jewellery,** some patterns of which are unique, is well finished, both in gold and silver: the principal articles are *rings, salvers, tea decocters* or *súlkí,* and *súraies* or wine, water, or scent bottles; but the smiths are so clever that they are able to imitate almost any design, however elaborate. The quality of the *swords* and *firearms* is very superior, and therefore famous. *Wine* was extensively made in former times, and the manufacture of *cider* and of *perry,* as previously mentioned, was attempted in 1864, but, owing chiefly to the bad quality of the casks, it proved a failure. *Paper* is also a Government manufacture; it is of excellent quality—smooth, strong, and like parchment, and is chiefly made from *bhang*—the Indian hemp—at Naoshera, near Srinagar.

26. Kashmir, like British India, is under a foreign

* See Appendix No. 2.

Government.

yoke, and its government is administered by a Viceroy or Governor appointed by His Highness *Ranbeer Singh*, the Maharajah of Jamoo, of whose dominions, as previously stated, it forms a portion. *Wazeer Punnoo* is the present Governor; he has filled the office off and on for many years. His usual residence is at *Sher Garhi*, or the palace at Srinagar; and he is assisted by the following high officers, viz.:—

Financial and Revenue Commissioner, or Nagdi and Jinsi.
Judge of Chief Court.
Accountant-General.
Superintendent of Shawls.
Judge of the Civil Court.

Laws.

27. The *Hindú Code of Laws* is in force, and the penalties, now-a-days at least, are not severe. The *Maharajah* is personally very popular, and although complaints against the conduct of the subordinate officers, especially from Mahomedans, occasionally reach the ears of visitors, it is believed that the State is upon the whole well governed. Serious crimes are rare, and thefts are not of common occurrence; public order is well preserved, and the security of person, life, and property is very striking. A man, woman, or child may travel all over the country without fear of being molested, and European ladies

and children may not only do the same, but depend upon every assistance and attention. The system of government, indeed, appears well adapted to the present condition of the people. The liberal tendencies of the present Maharajah are fully shown in the establishment of schools, colleges, and dispensaries in various parts of his territories, and there is little doubt that counsel judiciously tendered by the Indian Government will be always well received and readily adopted for the further benefit of his subjects.

Administrative divisions.

28. The administration of the province has lately been organized upon the *British* plan; it has been divided into six *wazárits* or districts, to each of which has been appointed a *wazeer wazárit* or deputy commissioner, and each of those again divided into a variable number of *tehsils* or parishes, according to the following list.

Administrative Divisions of Kashmir.

No.	Wazárits or Districts.	Names of present Wazeer Wazárits or Deputy Commissioners.	Tehsils.	Chief Town.	Tappas.
1	Sherkhás or Srinagar.	Pandit Rámju, adopted son of Pandit Rájkák, of Srinagar.	1. Yech. 2. Woolar. 3. Nágám and Aragám. 4. Phak. 5. Vihu. 6. Echun.	Srinagar. Pámpoor.	

Administrative Divisions of Kashmir—(Continued.)

No.	Wazárits or Districts.	Names of present Wazeer Wazárits or Deputy Commissioners.	Tehsils.	Chief Town.	Tappas.
2	Anant Nág ..	Misar Rahdú, of Jamoo.	1. Bringh. 2. Khaurpara & Martund. 3. Dachiupára. 4. Shábabád. 5. Anantnán.	Anant Nág. Shábabad. Bijbehára.	
3	Shupiyan ...	Janki Dass, of Jamoo.	1. Shupiyan. 2. Arwan. 3. Diosur. 4. Rámpathri.	Shupiyan.	
4	Pattan ...	Pundit Bálik Rám, of Srinagar.	1. Bangil. 2. Lál & Pruspore. 3. Birwa and Máchiháma. 4. Dúnsú.	Pattan.	
5	Kamráj ...	Máhta Sher Singh, of Rájori.	1. Hammel. 2. Kroohin. 3. Ootár Machipora. 4. Quiháma Loláb and Zainagir.	Sopoor. Báramúla.	
6	Múzufferabád	Goolám Alli Sháh, of Jamoo.	Múzufferabád.	Múzufferabad.	1. Kotla. 2. Gohóri. 3. Dópatta. 4. Katháhi. 5. Karná.
			Chikár ...	Chikár ...	1. Danna. 2. Chikár. 3. Ooir. 4. Búnyár.

29. No budget is published by the Kashmir Government, and the income and expenditure are therefore not exactly known. The former, however, probably amounts to about forty *lakhs* of rupees, or £400,000 per annum; it is derived from numerous sources, as trade licenses, import and export duties, and others; but the chief of them are the tax on shawls and other manufactures, and the proceeds of the sale of the Government share of the land produce—for the soil is considered the property of the ruler, who, as in native states generally, claims two-thirds of the crops, the remainder being retained by the cultivator. The produce of the lakes and rivers —as the *singhára* or water-nut, and fish—is also deemed royal property, and a considerable income is derived from this source also. The chief items of *expenditure* are the army, roads, public buildings, and charges relating to law and religion

Revenue.

30. There is a considerable trade carried on between *Eastern Túrkestán* and the *Panjáb*, in which Kashmir shares to a large extent. The Indian Government have long been desirous of increasing and regulating this traffic, and in furtherance of this object a Mission, headed by *Sir T. D. Forsyth, C.B., K.C.S.I.* of the Bengal Civil Service, was deputed in 1870 to visit that part of *Central*

Trade and commerce.

Asia, and to penetrate, if possible, as far as *Yarkand;* but owing chiefly to the absence of the *Ruler of Kashgar* —the *Kushbegi*—it was not completely successful. A commercial treaty was however concluded with the Maharajah of Jamoo and Kashmir,—who, by-the-way, is not yet an enthusiastic *free trader*, and whose coffers are still greatly enriched by the proceeds of state monopolies,—by which, amongst other things, it was provided that an officer of the *British Government*, and one of that of *Kashmir*, should form a *Joint Commission*, and reside every year during the hot season at *Leh*, the capital of *Ladák*, and on the high road to *Yarkand*, for the purpose of settling all matters connected with the safety, comfort, and convenience of the traders. A copy of this *Treaty*, as well as *Tables of Trade*, will be found in *Appendices* 3 and 4.

A second and more complete and scientific Mission, also under Sir D. Forsyth, was sent to Yarkand in 1873, and a commercial treaty was successfully concluded with the Ameer of Kashgar.*

Military forces.

31. The Maharajah keeps up a considerable army; the men are chiefly *Dogras*, but there are other classes also, as *Gilghitis*, *Astoris*, and others. Their pay is liberal; they

* This has been followed by the importation of a large quantity of English goods by the Central Asian Company, the results of which are not yet exactly known.

are dressed and drilled after the *British* fashion, and their officers, who are almost all native gentlemen, use the English words of command. The *artillery* does not muster, perhaps, more than thirty guns of all kinds; the *cavalry* arm is also small, and is employed chiefly as His Highness's Escort; but the *infantry* probably numbers more than 20 *battalions* of from 600 to 800 strong, and they are dispersed throughout all parts of the Maharajah's dominions, including *Ladák*, *Gilhit*, and other States.

History of Kashmir.

32. Kashmir has been a place of celebrity from the earliest times, and there are historians who carry its history back to the *Creation*, one of them affirming that it was visited by Adam after the *Fall*. *Moses* is said to have died there, and the descendants of *Seth* are stated to have reigned over it for 1,100 years. The period of the *Deluge* is indicated by the legend regarding the dessication of the Valley by the divine sage *Kashuf* or *Kusyapa*. *Solomon* is said to have visited it, and to have introduced the worship of the *One God*, which long continued the prevailing faith; but it was succeeded by idolatry, which, with one or two intervals of *Bhuddism*, prevailed until about the beginning of the 14th century.

It appears to have been usually governed by its

Its ancient rulers.

native Kings; but from about 150 to 100 B.C. it was ruled by *Tartar Princes;* and about 1015 A.D., *Mahmud* of *Ghuzni* took possession of it, and held it and the surrounding mountains for some time. In 1305, again, it was invaded from *Tibet*, the Hindu King *Sena Deva* fled the country, forfeited his throne, and was succeeded by *Ranjpoee*, son of *Yuftan*, King of Tibet, who is said to have been converted to Islam, and to have assumed the name of *Sadarúdín.* On the death of his widow *Koterdevi*, his minister *Shah Mir* ascended the throne under the name of *Shumshudin* (1341), and he is usually considered the first Mahomedan King of Kashmir, the alleged conversion of *Ranjpoee* being disputed by the Hindus. The names of his descendants and successors are *Jamshed* and *Ullahúdín*, his sons; and *Shahábudín*, his grandson (1356), who was one of the most fanatical of Moslems. *Kutabudin*, brother of the latter, was the father of *Sikunder*, surnamed *Butshikan*, one of the most famous iconoclasts of history, and by whom many of the ancient temples in Kashmir were either mutilated or destroyed. *Zinulabudin* or *Badshah*, the Great King (1423), who reigned fifty-three years, was a poet, artist, and sportsman—an encourager of architecture, literature, and the arts; he introduced weaving, paper-

Its independent Mahomedan kings.

making, glass-making, book-binding, and the celebrated *papier-maché* work, and his name is still a *household word* throughout the valley. *Mohamed Shah*, his great grandson, succeeded him in 1487, but his title to the throne was disputed by his uncle, *Futteh Shah*, and civil strife of many years' duration was the consequence. In 1536 *Kaji*, a member of the *Chák* family—whose tombs are numerous in and around Srinagar—taking advantage of these intestine struggles, seized the throne, and although he permitted the sons of *Mahomed Shah* to retain their dignity and to coin in their own names, he still remained the actual ruler of the country. He signally defeated the army of Mirza Kamràn, brought to terms an army of *Kashgarris*, which, under *Syed Khan* and *Mirza Hyder*, had invaded Kashmir, and penetrated as far as the *Lar* Pergunnah, in the Sind valley (1537), and successfully resisted the armies of the Emperor *Humayun*. In 1540, however, he was at length defeated by *Mirza Hyder*, the foster-brother of that Emperor, and who then became the Governor of the province; but an insurrection shortly afterwards occurred, in which he was defeated and slain. The *Chák* family then returned to power and occupied the throne. *Ghazi Khan* began to reign in 1556, and he repelled the successive invasions of the *Moguls*, *Tartars*, *Kashgarris*, *Turks*, and other

The Cháks.

enemies—*Yusaf Shah* in 1580 and *Yakub Khan*, his son, in 1585. After a brave and prolonged resistance, the latter was eventually defeated by *Kasim Khan*, the *admiral* of the Emperor *Akbar*, who then (1587) finally annexed the province to the Mogul Empire. From that time until now it has always formed an appanage of some neighbouring State, and its affairs have been administered by a *Subadar* or Governor appointed therefrom.

The Mogul Emperors.

34. It remained a portion of the *Mogul Empire* from 1587 to 1753, during which period (166 years) it was the frequent summer retreat of the Kings of Delhi. *Akbar* visited it after its conquest in 1588, and also in 1592, and 1599; *Jehangir* and the lovely *Noormehal* visited it several years successively, and death overtook him at *Barramgalla* while on his way thither; his illustrious successors *Sháh Jehan* and *Aurangzebe*, and also others, visited it often. The Mogul Emperors have left their traces in the large and beautiful *serais* or inns which are built at frequent intervals along the *Bhimber* and *Pir Panjal road*, and in the numerous though ruined *gardens*, *groves*, *baths*, and *palaces* which still adorn the valley. The *Mogul Governors*, as had been customary with the ancient Kings of Kashmir, used to reside for six months out of the Valley, on account of the cold; *Ali Mardán Khán*,

the most magnificent of them, did the same, and the expenses of each of his trips are said to have exceeded a *lakh* of rupees, or £10,000 sterling; from which it may be inferred that the country was far richer than at the present time.

Pathan Rulers.

35. The invasion of *Nádir Sháh* in 1739, and his capture, massacre, and sacking of *Delhi*, precipitated the fall of the already tottering *Mogul Empire.* The Governors of some of its provinces, particularly its more distant ones, began to relax in their allegiance and dream of establishing themselves as independent princes. Such was the case in Kashmir, where, in 1740, the Governor *Abdúl Barkat*, a native chief, defied the imperial authority, and continued to govern the province in his own name. On the accession of the Emperor *Ahmed Shah* in 1752, however, a new Mogul Governor was sent there, but being opposed by *Abdúl Kásim*, son of the abovenamed *Abdúl Barkat*, he sought the aid of *Nádir Sháh's* successor, *Ahmed Shah, Abdali*, who, in 1753, despatched a force under *Abdúlla Khán* to assist him. The latter however, seized the country, annexed it to the *Dourâni Empire*, which already included the provinces of *Peshawar*, *Lahore*, and *Mooltán*, and after having plundered it to the extent of about a *crore* of rupees—a million sterling—he returned to Lahore to lay his spoils at his

master's feet, leaving the *Rajah Sookh Jewan* as his deputy. It remained a portion of this empire from 1753 to 1819, during which period (66 years) no less than fourteen Governors ruled over it. Their allegiance was however by no means always steadfast, for several of them asserted, and for a time maintained, their independence; as *Amir Khán Sher Jewan* in 1769, *Asad Khán* in 1783—the tyrant of whom it is written that "he killed men as though they were birds,"—*Abdulla Khan* in 1795, and his son *Atta Mahomed Khan* in 1800. It was visited by *Sháh Zemán* in 1795, and *Futteh Khán Barakzai*, aided by *Ranjit Singh's* auxiliary force under *Mokim Chand*, himself proceeded there in 1813 to recover it from the hands of the rebel Governor, *Atta Mahomed Khán*. *Jehándar Khán*, brother of the latter, was at this time Governor of Attock, which, like Kashmir, was also a *Pathan* possession. The brothers intended by appropriating these to form a little kingdom for themselves; their object was however frustrated; but when *Futteh Khan* was approaching to besiege the Fort of Attock, the traitor Governor sold it to *Ranjit Singh*, whereupon the former withheld the subsidy he had promised to pay the latter for his aid in recovering Kashmir, and a declaration of war ensued. In the following year *Ranjit Singh* headed an army to invade Kashmir; he was however unsuccessful, but in 1819 he renewed the attempt, and on the 5th July of that year his General, *Misser Diwan Chand,* defeated the Pathan Governor *Jabbar Khan* at *Chotipur,* near *Shupiyan* and annexed it to his master's dominions, which already included nearly all the *Punjab,* and most of the adjoining hill states.

Sikh Rulers.

36. Thus, after a lapse of nearly five centuries, Kashmir again passed under the sway of a Hindu sovereign. The rule of the Pathans had been neither mild nor beneficial, and the change appears to have been agreeable to the people. To the Sikhs generally its conquest was a proud event, so much so indeed that their war cry "bolo wáh gúrújiká khalsa! bolo sreewáh gúrújiki fatah!" is said, though doubtfully, to be composed of letters corresponding to the date and the year of the Hindu era—*Sambat* 1876—on which it occurred. *Ranjit Singh* never visited this his fairest province himself; he died in 1839, and the dissolution of his kingdom, chiefly from failure of his line, speedily commenced. It continued, however, to be attached to the Punjab until the conclusion of the *Sutlej Campaign* and the British occupation of Lahore, shortly after which it was assigned, by a treaty dated 16th March, 1846, to *Golab Singh,* the *Maharajah of Jamoo.* From *Ranjit Singh's* conquest in 1819 to that date—about twenty-seven years—

the number of its Sikh Governors was no less than ten, and the following are their names:—*Moti Ram*, 1819; *Harri Singh*, 1820; *Moti Ram* (again), 1822; *Gurmukh Singh*, 1823; *Kirpa Ram*, 1824; *Bhumma Singh*, 1830; *Prince Shere Singh*, 1831; *Colonel Mean Singh*, 1833; *Golam Mohy-u-din*, 1842; and *Shaikh Emam-u-din*, 1845. The year 1824 is celebrated for the terrible *earthquakes* in the valley, 1838 for the destructive *floods*, and 1843 for the *epidemic* of cholera, which was so general and so fatal that more than 20,000 persons are said to have died in Srinagar alone.

Its present Sovereign.

37. The present Sovereign of Kashmir is *Ranbeer Singh*, son of *Golab Singh*, who died 2nd of August, 1857; he was born 15th June, 1830, and at once succeeded to the throne on his father's death. He is a *Rajpút* of the highest caste and has four sons—the *Mean Sahib, Pertab Singh*, (born 23rd May, 1850), *Mean Ram Singh, Mean Umur Singh* and *Mean Lachman Singh*. His usual residence is at *Jamoo*—the home of his ancestors—but he generally spends a month or two in the *Kashmir Valley* during the hot season. In religion he is a Dogra, a sect of Hindus. He is a great encourager of all religious works, and is understood to be much influenced by the advice and teachings of the numerous *pandits* and other *Brahmins* by whom he is surrounded, and

to whom he is extremely liberal. At the same time he is also a munificent patron of education, and indeed bids fair to take a foremost place amongst the most enlightened Princes of *Her Majesty's Indian Dominions.* His present representative in Kashmir is *Wazeer Pannoo*, who has off and on, as previously stated, filled the office of Governor for many years past.

Religion.

38. The religion of Kashmir has been very often changed; it was probably one of the first places colonized by the *Aryan* race after they descended from the plains of Central Asia, and here they practised the *nága* or *snake worship*, which, as shown in *Ferguson's* "Tree and Serpent Worship," was one of the earliest forms of idolatry. *Buddhism* was introduced by *Asoka* about 250 B.C., and he and his grandson *Jalako* especially have left their marks upon the *Takht-i-Súlimán*, *Pandritan*, and many other places, where ruined temples and other buildings may still be found. *Hinduism* was introduced by *Abhimanyú* about 75 B.C., and it flourished there for centuries in its highest form; its *pandits* were very famous; their eminence in learning is often alluded to in the *Máhabárat*, the *Bhágavata*, and other *Sanskrit* works, and their descendants, as previously stated, hold a fair position even now in the world of *Aryan* letters. *Mohamedanism* was established about 1356 A.D. by

Syed Ali Hamadáni and his son *Mir Mohamed,* who, during the reign of *Shahab-u-din,* arrived in Kashmir with a train of more than 1,000 fugitive disciples from Persia.* A terrible crusade ensued against the Hindus, who are said to have been forcibly converted to the new faith, and the fierce zeal of some of the kings, notoriously that of *Sikander*—surnamed the *idol breaker* —has made their names infamous in history; they waged a deadly war against all architecture which attested the existence of another creed, and, as the traveller witnesses throughout Kashmir, beautiful remains of sculpture have been devoted to the lowest and meanest purposes. Mohamedanism is still professed by the great majority of the inhabitants, but since their conquest by *Ranjit Singh* in 1819, Hinduism has again been greatly favored, especially that form of it which is the creed of the reigning dynasty.

39. The antiquities of Kashmir consist of its *noble ruins* and its numerous *ancient coins.* Of the former, Vigne says there are not less than about seventy; but the chief are those at *Martand, Awantipoor, Rájdainbul, Pándritan,* the building on the summit of the *Takht-i-Suliman,* and the

Antiquities.

* A fakir named *Bulbul Shah,* a native of Tibet, is said to have been the *first* Mohamedan who appeared in Kashmir. The alleged conversion of *Ranjpoee* is attributed to him; and his tomb is still standing on the right bank of the Jhelam, a little below the Ali Kadal, Srinagar.

little temple at *Payech*—the gem of all. The style of these ruins is original and peculiar to the country, their dates and uses are not exactly known, and they have long excited the keenest interest of archæologists. The natives attribute them superstitiously to the *Pandus*, whom they regard as a race of giants, of enormous strength and allied to the gods, but who were, in fact, five brothers, the sons of *Pánd*, a Hindu king of the Lunar race, who reigned in the city of *Astunpur*, on the Ganges, some ten or twelve centuries before the Christian era; they are supposed to have wandered over a part of Central Asia, and to have settled for a time in Kashmir. The buildings were however probably used as temples, and they indicate a degree of greatness, resource, and prosperity, which contrasts painfully with the present condition of meanness and wretchedness which is observable throughout the greater portion of the province. The subject of *coins* is one deserving of deeper study. Many years ago *General A. Cunningham* made a collection, and some were of the time of its native rajahs—those who preceded the Mahomedan kings. There is reason, however, to believe that others still more interesting may be found; and as this eminent antiquarian has again lately visited Kashmir, an account of his further researches may be eagerly and confidently looked for.

Literature.

40. The literature of Kashmir, like its architecture, has sadly fallen into decay; it boasts of three works however, which, from their intrinsic merits, are of the highest value; they are the *Rájtaringini*, the *Vrihet Katha*, and the *Nila Parana*. The *first*—the one great historical work in Sanskrit—has been translated by *Major Fryer*, under the title "Histoire de Kashmir," in which he gives the Sanskrit text of the original, with copious notes, and a dissertation on the Valley, ethnographical, historical, and geological;—and the *second* has been reprinted and edited by *Brockhaus* in German. The *Rev. J. Long*, who visited Kashmir in 1871, and who hoped to have made a large collection of *Sanskrit* MSS. found about fourteen new *nataks* or dramas which he proposes to have translated, as they will doubtless throw much light upon the social condition of the Hindus at the time they were written. The MSS., are written upon the bark of a tree, and he saw some which he had good reason to believe were 800 years old and in a good state of preservation—a surprising thing, as he says, when we consider the crusade waged against all Hindu literature by the ruthless Pathan conquerors, who levelled temples and consumed libraries. He ascertained that it was true that only two original copies of the *Rajtaringini* were extant, and the pandit was pointed out to

him who lent one copy to *Professor H. H. Wilson*, who wrote the celebrated article upon it which may be found in Vol. XV. of the *Asiatic Researches* or *Transactions of the Society*, 1825. It may here be stated that it is chiefly from that ancient work that the principal facts of the foregoing historical sketch are derived, and which brings this chapter to its close.

CHAPTER II.

ROUTES TO SRINAGAR, THE CAPITAL.

Accessibility of Kashmir.

The foregoing is a slight sketch of the province of Kashmir, which has been poetically called an *Earthly Paradise*, and which possesses such varied attractions alike to the lover of nature, the invalid, the artist and photographer, and the antiquarian, as well as to the angler and sportsman (*vide* Appendix No. 5). Its popularity is annually increasing. *Americans* and *Germans* are now amongst the visitors, and the tide of foreigners is likely to swell as greater facilities are afforded in travelling from *Central Europe* and *Southern Russia*, so that ere long Kashmir may not improbably form a part of *le grand tour*, which even in the days of our grandfathers was so limited. The *Panjab Northern State Railway* is open as far as Gújrát, which is the principal starting point from the Panjab, and about 70 miles, or a night's journey, above Lahore, the capital of the province, and which is now within three or four days' reach by railway of Bombay and Calcutta. The journey from London to Bombay occupies about twenty-one days, and costs, with first class accommodation, about £65; from *London* to *Calcutta* about 25 days, and costs about £75. The whole journey from *London* to *Lahore* may therefore be accomplished within a month, and for about £100.

Advantages over Indian hill stations.

To Anglo-Indians having a couple of months or so at their disposal, *Kashmir* is preferable to any hill station in India; it presents a far greater variety of scenery—hill and dale, wood and water, and ranges of climate to suit any constitution; it is far more extensive, and excursions can be made in all directions to lovely valleys, beautiful mountain meadows, or to snowy glaciers, and thus if desirable constant change may be obtained; it is not only cheaper, but has great advantages as a health resort, especially for delicate women, and as every one takes his tents and camp furniture, he is independent of houses, and may lead a gipsy life, roaming about from day to day, and seeking new spots of charming and ever varying landscape. Most people prefer visiting it in the early months from middle of April to middle of June, which is perhaps the best time; others from middle of August to middle of October. The intervening period is least to be preferred, especially for marching there or back, on account of the heat and heavy rains which then prevail.

Authorised routes.

Srinagar is the capital of the province, and as most visitors make for that place first, it may be taken as the *Terminus* of the various routes, of which there are several, as may be seen on Montgomerie's *Kashmir Route Map.* Only four of them however are authorized or public, and the Supreme Government positively forbids any of its officers to travel by any others, unless special permission is previously obtained through the *Punjab Government.* The authorised routes are as follows, *viz* :—

I. Gújrát and Pir Panjál.

II. Gújrát and Púnch.

III. Ráwal Pindi and Marri.

IV. Ráwal Pindi and Abbottabad.

They are all marked in the accompanying *map* which has been compiled chiefly from the excellent *Jamoo and Kashmir map.* The *easiest* is perhaps the *Rawal Pindi and Marri* route, next the *Gújrat and Pir Punjal,* the most difficult is the *Gújrat and*

Púnch. The *Gújrat and Pir Panjal* route is the *grandest;* the *Rawal Pindi and Abbottabad* the *hottest,* owing to its generally southern aspect. *Jampans* and *dandies* can pass along them all, and they may all be ridden over, except some portion of the *Gújrat and Púnch* route, in which walking is safer.

Arrangements for visitors.

His Highness the Maharajah of *Kashmir* has caused very liberal and complete arrangements to be made for the comfort and convenience of visitors; indeed they are treated more as *guests* than as ordinary *travellers,* and in moving about they bear in mind that they are in a foreign state, belonging to a friendly and powerful Feudatory of the British Government; they are also disposed to make allowances for any differences in a system of Government, which is naturally less enlightened than their own; and at the same time to treat the ministers and other officials with suitable courtesy and consideration, more especially as they are generally civil and very attentive. The ROADS, especially those along the routes Nos. 1 and 3, have already been very much improved, and are being, at a heavy outlay, made still more easy. There is a BUNGALOW or some kind of building at every stage along all the authorised routes, and out-offices for horses and servants, as well as an encamping ground. In *British* territory the bungalows are furnished, servants are attached to them, and rent is charged at the usual rates; the *Kashmirian* ones however are only partly furnished; there are no efficient servants, and as yet no rent is required for using them. Ordinary PROVISIONS as milk, butter, rice, ghee, flour, fowls, eggs and other country articles, are procurable at every stage, and on the *Rawal Pindi and Marri* route *khansamahs* have this year been appointed under a contractor, and are provided with cooking utensils, &c., as well as beer, soda water, spirits, and a few European stores; this speculation is however not likely to prove successful, and visitors are recommended not to rely upon it, at least for the present. There is also an official who arranges for COOLIES and other kinds of CARRIAGE, to whom a day's notice should be sent; the rates of supplies and carriage are uniform for the season, they are much the same as those prevailing in the adjoining British Districts, and an authentic schedule of them is posted at every stage. The supply of baggage mules and ponies is limited and rather uncertain, but coolies are usually abundant; as however they are generally labourers drawn away, and often at great inconvenience, from their fields, they should be paid and dismissed as quickly as possible after delivering their loads, and always if practicable in the visitor's presence. The rates of carriage, &c., are as follows :—

Saddle ponies	... ...	Re. 1	per stage.
Baggage do. or mules	... ...	As. 8	do.
Coolies, or porters	... ...	As. 4	do.
Kuhars or bearers	... ...	As. 6	do.

Requisites.

The issue of passes by the Kashmir Government has been discontinued, but an officer desirous of visiting the country must first obtain LEAVE from the local Government under which he is serving or from His Excellency the Commander-in-Chief, as the case may be (*vide* G. O. C. C. No. 63 of 1870), and he should provide himself with a copy of the RULES for the guidance of Officers and others visiting Kashmir (*vide* Appendix No. 6). In undertaking the trip, it should be remembered that the same arrangements are necessary as those for ordinary marching, except that, as the road lies through the mountains, and carriage is somewhat scarce, the baggage should be as light as possible. As to TENTS and FURNITURE, the most convenient kind of the former for married people, is the small size *Swiss cottage*; a *Soubadar's* tent or *Shouldari*, is suitable for bachelors, one of which for the use of the kitchen and servants, is equally desirable for both; the *tables*, *chairs*, and *bedsteads* should be made to fold up; the *dishes plates*, &c., should be enamelled iron-ware, and the *cooking vessels* nested or of the Bombay pattern. The whole equipment for one person will cost about Rs. 100. A supply of STORES as beer, wine, tea, sugar, candles, fine flour, carbonate of soda (for scons or soda *chappatis*) rice, potatoes, salt, spices, pastilles of myrrh or frankincense, carbolic acid oil, and chloralum (for purposes of fumigation or disinfection) and any other individual necessaries should be laid in at Lahore or Gújrát, Ráwal Pindi or Marri, sufficient for the journey to *Srinagar*, where there are several good shops, at which all kinds of European stores, as beer, wine, spirits, oilman's stores, lemonade, soda water, &c., are procurable, and at reasonable prices. A small stock of *clothes* will suffice, as cheap woollen materials are readily procured at Srinagar, a complete suit of gentlemen's clothes of *passú*, made to order, costs only from 5 to 8 or Rs. 10, and ladies' and children's dresses, boots, and shoes, are equally cheap. The visitor is recommended to provide himself with a few other BOOKS relating to the country, a tolerably complete list of which will be found in the preface, also the map of *Jamoo and Kashmir*, a *thermometer*, an *aneroid barometer*, a universal *sun dial*, and especially Moore's "*Lalla Rookh*," all of which will be found useful. For PACKING clothes, cooking utensils, stores, and such articles, *kiltas*-deep wicker-baskets, covered with thin leather, are the best of all, as the Kashmiri coolies carry their loads like our London coal porters, on their backs or shoulders, and not upon their heads, as Indian coolies generally do; pairs of *leathern trunks* or *boxes*, about 2 feet long, 1 foot broad, and 10 inches deep, are equally convenient for mules or coolies, as are also the *rakhtdans*, or leathern boxes made at Peshawar and Ráwal Pindi. A *waterproof sheet* for the bedding is indispensable, and a strong *portable bath* equally so. SERVANTS, if numerous, are a great encumbrance ; a *khitmutgar* and a *bhistie* are sufficient for a bachelor, and married people should take as few as possible, especially of the female sex. *Bhisties* and *dhobies* may generally be engaged at Srinagar, and occasionally an *ayah;* some of the boatmen now and then act as *bearers* and *khitmutgars*, but they are more suitable for bachelors than for married people. As regards MONEY, the Indian silver coins are readily taken at their full value throughout Kashmir; gold *mohurs* and sovereigns, currency notes, and money orders, are however only negotiable at Srinagar, and the two latter are subject to a discount of from two to five *per cent.* The visitor should therefore take as much silver coin as will last him to Srinagar, and the remainder of his money in gold, currency notes, or money orders, the last being made payable at the *Umritsur* Treasury; in this form also officers should have their *remittances* sent to them from their Regimental head-quarters. The *Kashmir coins* are chiefly silver and copper; of the *former* there are three kinds of rupees. The *nanak shahi*, worth 16 annas; the *chilki* now almost the only current one, worth 10 annas; and the *harri singhi*, worth only 8 annas; of the *latter* there is now only one kind, and called pice, 10 of which are equal to 1 anna; most of them are very rudely stamped, and considerably alloyed; but the new 10 anna *chilkis* are of a better shape and metal, and are readily taken in the Indian *bazars*. The POSTAL ARRANGEMENTS are in imitation of those of India; there is a regular mail between *Ráwal Pindi*, *Marri* and *Srinagar* throughout the season; all letters and other correspondence however require Kashmerian postage stamps in addition to the Indian ones. The *Postal Rules* will be found in Appendix No. 7.

Mode of travelling.

Many of the hardier sex prefer walking all the way in leather sandals or *chaplis*, and with the aid of an alpenstock, but most of them find, at least during the first few stages, that a RIDING PONY is a luxury if not a necessity, and it is therefore usual for visitors to provide themselves with one; they may be purchased at Lahore, Ráwal Pindi or Marri; the best kind is the *Yarkand* pony; next those of *Bokhara*, or *Cabul.* Good strong animals may also be hired at all the stages on routes Nos. 1 and 3 in Kashmirian territory, and they are most of them specially drafted from the large and numerous stables of the Maharajah. Ladies can also ride the whole way, but they usually travel in DANDIS or in JAMPANS, the former requiring 4 bearers, and the latter 6, for each stage; some take their *Jampanis* with them from Marri; children are usually carried in COTS, hung upon a pole which passes through an iron ring, upon upright pieces at each end. For WALKING in dry weather the *chaplis* or leather sandals, with brown leathern socks, are the easiest and most comfortable for the feet, and for both sexes; black leather, especially enamelled or glazed, should be carefully avoided for boots or shoes; the best and coolest kind is the *brown leather,* and the soles should always be thick and flat, on account of the usual roughness of the roads; for like reasons brown leathern gaiters are preferable to black ones. A GUIDE is always useful, and is recommended upon all occasions; an intelligent cooly, who knows the road, may be selected at the beginning of each stage to accompany the visitor, and carry a light load consisting, for instance, of *maps*, *books,* a few articles of *clothing* and some *refreshments ;* he can also show the short cuts to the pedestrian—the *pagdandis*, as they are called, being in general much more level than the road itself, as well as taking off many bad bits. A complete suit of *waterproof clothing* should always be at hand, especially during the months of July and August. An EARLY DINNER will generally be most convenient, both for visitors and their servants ; the spare baggage and kitchen establishment can then go on in the evening, and an early breakfast can be prepared the next morning, either half way on the road, or at the next stage as may be most preferred; in the latter case a couple of eggs with a cup of milk or tea, and some soda scons had better be taken before starting. *During the first two or three marches* there is usually a little trouble and confusion, but the servants very soon get into training, and afterwards things glide on quite smoothly and pleasantly.

Having offered the above few HINTS TO VISITORS, a detailed description of the various routes may now be given.

1. Gujrat and Pir Panjal Route.

This is the principal route, and though not perhaps the easiest, it is the most interesting in historical associations and the grandest for scenery; is usually open from the beginning of May until about the end of October, the *Pir Panjal Pass* being in the *interim* snow. It was used by the Mogul Emperors in their frequent visits to the valley—the change to which from being cooped up within the burning walls of *Delhi* or *Agra*, in a naked country, parched by a cloudless summer sky, they so much enjoyed. It is therefore called the *Imperial Road*, and along the whole way, at intervals of a few miles, may still be seen the ruins of magnificent *serais* or *inns*; which were built (mostly by the Governor *Ali Mardan Khan*, and in the time of *Shah Jehan*), as resting-places for themselves and their numerous followers. It is stated that in *Aurangzebe's* last visit he was escorted by an army of 10,000 foot, 30,000 horse, 70 heavy guns, 50 field-pieces, a stately line of elephants, his *zenana*, and Bernier, his physician. It is also the chief commercial highway between the Panjab and Kashmir, and merchandize is carried by coolies, mules, and ponies, and as far as *Barramgalla*, by bullocks.

2. GUJRAT is the starting point from the Punjab; it is a pretty station on the *Grand Trunk Road*, about 70 miles above Lahore, with which—except the break across the *Chenab* river—it is now connected

by railway. There is a very good *bungalow* for travellers, and *camp furniture* and *stores* are procurable; but as the supply is at present rather uncertain, it is better, to purchase them at Lahore. The number of stages between *Gujrat* and *Srinagar* is 15, and the following is a list of them :—

Stages on the Gujrat and Pir Panjal Route.

No.	Name.	Distance.	Average time occupied exclusive of halting	
1	Gujrat to	Miles.	Hours.	
2	Dowlatnagar...			
3	Kotla ...			
4	Bhimber ...	28½		
5	Saidabad ...	15	6	
6	Naoshera ...	12½	4½	
7	Changas ...	13¾	6	
8	Rajaori ...	14	6½	
9	Thanna Mandi	14	6½	
10	Baramgalla ...	10½	6	
11	Poshiana ...	8	3½	
12	Aliabad Serai	11	5½	
13	Hirapoor ...	12	4½	
14	Shupiyan ...	8	3	
15	Ramoo ...	11	4	
	Srinagar ...	18	6	

3. GUJRAT TO BHIMBER.—The distance is about 28½ miles; the road, though unmetalled, is easy, and lies along the plains; the intermediate stages are

Dowlatnagar and *Kotla*, but the whole distance is usually accomplished in one journey, either by *dhooly dak* or by *stage cart;* the former is the more common, and the cost for one person, including the use and return hire of the dhooly, is about 10 rupees; by the stage cart the fare for one seat is 10 rupees, and for three seats or a whole cart 21 rupees. BHIMBER is a considerable town within the Maharajah's territories; it is situated near the right bank of a stream of the same name, and surrounded, except towards the south, by low and densely-wooded hills, which are only three or four miles distant. There are two *bungalows for visitors*;* both are situated on an open space, a little to the south-east of the town; they are built of stone raised about two feet above the ground and each contains four rooms, two large and two small. The Kashmiri officials will generally be found very civil and attentive to visitors. There is an old Mogul *serai* in the middle of the town, also the ruins of a fort. The last legitimate rajah, *Sultan Khan*, was taken prisoner by *Ranjit Singh* and sent to Rihursi, where, by order of *Golab Singh*, his eyes were afterwards put out with a red hot needle. The

* Some of the *Bungalows* along this Route and those of Nos. 2 and 4, have been altered since this Hand-Book was first written; in all other respects however the descriptions will, it is believed, still be found accurate.

fort upon the hill about 8 miles to the east was built by *Dhihan Singh*, brother of Golb Singh, and a favorite and powerful minister of Ranjit Singh.

4. BHIMBER TO SAIDABAD.—*Distance* 15*m*. *Time* 6*h*.

Road.—The range called the *Aditak*, the first of the four which intervene between the plains of the Panjab and those of Kashmir, has to be crossed about the middle of this march. The road, after skirting the town, leads down to the stream, which is about 30 yards wide, and its sandy bed is fordable; after passing through some fields it is again reached, but its bed is now stony, and after fording it about eight miles, the path turns to the left, up a narrow but very pretty valley—in which there is a small stream which has to be forded about ten times—to the foot of the *Aditak*, which may be regarded as the stepping stone to the Great Himalayas. The ascent is about 2½ miles long; the path averages about 8 feet wide; the lower portion is tolerably easy, but the upper is rather steep and rough; some parts are sandy, whilst others consist of bare, smooth, and somewhat slippery sandstone rocks, locally called *boosa*. There are a few trees upon this side of the ridge, amongst which are some pines, and here and there is an open grassy spot. On the top of the ridge, which is about 1,000 feet above the plains, there is a custom-house and a few other buildings, and in clear weather it commands a most beautiful and extensive view of the plains on one side, and the Saidabad valley and the distant snowy *Pir Panjal* mountains on the other. The descent on the other side is about a mile long; the path is winding, now and then rather steep, and in some places rough and narrowed by rocks on either side; trees, chiefly pines, are very numerous, as is usually the case on the northern sides of these mountains, and there are two or three open spaces covered with grass. From the bottom of the ridge the road leads across some high and cultivated land, then down to the right bank of a large stream whose rocky bed contains many a deep pool abounding in fish; it shortly afterwards turns to the left, to a ford across a small stream, and thence leads through the fields to Saidabad, which is about four miles from the foot of the ridge. SAIDABAD is a very small village on the right bank of a mountain stream, in the centre of a richly cultivated plain only a few miles broad, and surrounded by low and thickly-wooded hills. The *bungalow* is a good stone building just beyond the village, and near the ruins of a very dilapidated *serai;* it is on the same plan as those at Bhimber, but rather larger.

About a quarter of a mile to the north-east is the *Samani Serai*, built by Akber or Jehangir; it is a very fine building and in a fair state of preservation.

5. SAIDABAD TO NOASHERA. *Distance* 12½*m.* *Time* 4½*h.*

Road.—The range called *Kaman Goshi* has to be crossed in this march; the path at first leads along the banks of the stream, which has to be forded several times; it then winds through fields, which are intersected here and there by low grassy hills running right and left, and afterwards conducts to the foot of the range which is about five miles from *Saidabad.* It is not quite so high as the *Aditak*; the ascent is about a mile, and mostly over smooth, bare, and slate-colored rocks; the summit commands a splendid view, and there are a few huts, at one of which a draught of milk or water may usually be obtained: the descent is much longer; the path is generally smooth, but now and then rough and rather steep; and pines and other trees are numerous. NOASHERA is about three miles from the foot of the pass and over easy ground; it is a large stone-built town about 300 feet above the right bank of the *Tawi* river, and situated in a fine open plain several miles wide. The *bungalow* is situated in a large orchard called the *Baoli Bagh*, about a mile on this side of the town, and contains one middle-sized room above and three below. *Ranjit Singh* took the town in 1845: it contains a fine old Mogul *serai*, and the fort of *Jawir Singh* which is worth a visit.

6. Noashera to Changas.—*Distance* 13½*m.* *Time* 6*h.*

Road.—The route lies the whole way along the valley of the *Táwi*, which is usually not more than a mile wide, and bounded on both sides by low and beautifully wooded hills. There are two paths; the *lower* and shorter, preferred by the coolies, follows the bed of the river, and is very rough and only fit for walking; the *upper* or pony road passes mostly along the right bank of the river, and over about ten low spurs composed of rough slaty rocks: the scenery throughout is very fine. Changas is a very small and scattered village upon a table-land about 200 feet above the right bank of the Táwi; the *bungalow* is about a quarter of a mile from it, consists of three suites of rooms, overlooks the river, and commands a view of the *Pir Panjál*, not to be exceeded in grandeur by any in the valley.

7. Changas to Rajaori.—*Distance* 14*m.* *Time* 6½*h.*

Road.—The route, easy but hot, continues up the valley of the Tawi, and, as in the previous march, there are two paths, a *lower* or cooly road, and an *upper* or pony road; the latter passes along the right bank of the river and over about eight low spurs, similar to those in the previous stage. The first *chenár* or plane tree may be seen near the edge of the river, not far from the village of *Kular,* and about six miles from Changas. There are two old *serais* at *Moradpore,* which is about three miles further on; the usual path crosses the Táwi by a ford about three-quarters of a mile from RAJAORI: if, however, the river is very high, the visitor must continue along its right bank up to the town, which is also called RAMPORE. It is the largest along this route, very picturesquely situated at the foot of a low range of hills about 150 feet high, and overlooking the Táwi, whose bed is here exceedingly rough, and during the rains often impassable for several hours. The *bungalow* is on the left bank of the river, immediately opposite the town; it is an open pavilion, containing three small rooms, and situated in an enclosed garden about 80 yards square, in which there are some fountains and an aqueduct. Rajaori was an independent State in the 11th and 12th centuries under its own rajahs; its later rulers were Rajputs, who received their lands from *Aurungzebe,* and they then embraced Mahomedanism.

Golab Singh seized their territory in 1847, and they left for Central India, where they afterwards aided the English in the rebellion of 1857, and for which they subsequently obtained an estate in the Kangra district. The Mogul Emperors used to rest here in their progress to Káshmir, and there are several places worth visiting, as the Royal Cemetery at the back of the town, the *Amkhas, Musafirkhana,* Royal Palace, the temple, and the Bazar. A day's march to the east of Rajaori there are two hot springs which deposit sulphur.

8. Rajaori to Thanna Mandi.—*Distance* 14*m. Time* 6½*h.*

Road.—This is the easiest stage on this side of the Pir Panjál; the road still continues up the valley of the Táwi; both river and valley become gradually narrower, but the hills on each side become higher, and towards the end of the march the *Ruttan Pir* range is seen rising in front. A wide stream with a rough bed has to be forded about a mile from Rajaori; the village and old *serai* of *Futtipoor* are about a mile further on, and near *Leera Baoli,* about four miles beyond, the path leaves the river, approaching it again, and near an old *serai,* within a few hundred yards of Thanna Mandi. This is a small square and compact town or *bazar* built of round stones on the left bank of the Táwi, and at the mouth of the valley in which this river rises. It forms a depôt for the salt and various other articles passing to and from the Panjab. *Khâji Chák*, King of Kashmir, is said to have died here after his flight before *Mirza Hyder*. The *bungalow* is situated on the hillside above the right bank of the stream overlooking the *Mandi;* it is double-storied; the upper contains six moderate sized rooms, the lower is only fit for stables.

9. THANNA MANDI TO BARAMGALLA.—*Distance* 10½*m. Time* 6*h.*

Road.—The *Ruttan Pir* range has to be crossed in this march, the first half of which is a continuous but tolerably easy ascent, the other a similar descent. About a mile from Thanna Mandi, the Púnch road branches off to the left, and from this point to the small village of *Ajanabad,* high up on the right, the incipient *Táwi* has to be forded several times. The top of the pass is about 8,200 feet high; there are several huts upon it; it is about five miles from Thanna Mandi, and it commands a magnificent view. Near the end of the latter half of the march—the scenery of which is exquisite—a stream has to be crossed by a wooden bridge. BARAMGALLA is a small village in the territory of the Púnch Rajah, *Moti Singh;* it is situated upon a very small and elevated plateau, surrounded by very high and rugged mountains, and about 150 feet above the left bank of the *Sooran* river. The Emperor *Jehangir* died here of palsy, on his way to Kashmir, the fact of his death being kept concealed until his successor, *Shah Jehan* was proclaimed. Kashmir was his favourite residence; he spent thirteen summers there, and was anxious in his last moments to be carried to *Vernág*, but *Núrmahal*, his lovely and devoted wife, had the corpse conveyed to *Shàhdèra*, near Lahore, where she devoted the last twenty years of her life to erecting the magnificent mausoleum to his memory, which is still standing and is worthy of a visit. Of this Emperor's delights in Kashmir the poet Moore thus tenderly writes :—

So felt the magnificent Son of Akbar,
When from power and pomp and the trophies of war
He flew to that valley, forgetting them all,
With the Sight of the Haram, his young Nùrmahal.
When free and uncrown'd as the conqueror roved,
By the banks of the lake, with his only beloved,
He saw, in the wreaths she would playfully snatch
From the hedges, a glory his crown could not match,
And preferred in his heart the least ringlet that curl'd
Down her exquisite neck to the throne of the world.

The Baramgalla *bungalow* is a small and square mud *serai*, containing eight rooms, four large and four small, all opening into an interior courtyard. On the opposite bank of the river there is a fine old stone fort, occupying a lofty and most commanding situation. In winter the snow is said to lie 50 feet deep about here.

10. BARAMGALLA TO POSHIANA.—*Distance* 8*m*. *Time* 3½*h*.

Road.—The path lies up the deep and narrow valley of the *Sooran*, also called the *Chittapáni;* after a gentle ascent it descends to the bed of the river, which during the rains is a rapid torrent; it then continues for about five miles mostly along its stony bed, but crossing and re-crossing it about twenty-eight times by very roughly and simply constructed wooden bridges: about a mile or so from Poshiana, it ascends the right bank of the river and leads up to the village. There are several waterfalls along this march, but their number and beauty vary greatly with the season. The first and finest is situated in a nook on the right, about five minutes' walk from the *serai;* it is called *Nuri-Chasm*, and is about 70 feet high and imbedded in magnificent scenery: of the others, one is about half-way, and on the left bank, and there is another on the right, just before leaving the bed of the *Sooran.* POSHIANA is a very small village about half-way up the steep side of the lofty mountains. The *bungalow* is an old mud *serai,* now used as a cowshed; and visitors have to pitch their tents upon the flat roofs of the houses—the only available space. In wet weather shelter may be had for a small gratuity in one of the private huts, which is kept a little cleaner than the others for the use of visitors.

11. POSHIANA TO ALIABAD SERAI.—*Distance* 11*m.* *Time* 5½*h.*

Road.—The grand Pir Panjál range has to be crossed in this march; its formation is basaltic—an amygdaloid trap,—beautifully marked in some places; it is so called from a *fakir* who is buried in the pass, and at whose shrine offerings are made by native travellers. After an easy journey of half an hour along the mountain side, the path descends to the *Rámtakki*—an open space on the bank of the river, and sometimes used as an encamping ground; it then crosses the *Chittapáni* for the last time, and shortly leads to the *Nilána* valley, at the upper end of which begins the ascent of the Pir. *Chedikand* is a stone hut on the left, just after entering the *Nilána*; and *Rásikand* is another, about an hour's walk further on: they were built by the

Moguls as refuges for travellers during storms. The ascent of the pass is not so difficult as it seems when looking at the zig-zag path on the mountain side, for, though steep, the road is good. The top of the pass is about six miles distant from Poshiana; its elevation is about 11,500 feet, and it may be reached in about three hours; it is a fine grassy plateau about half a mile wide, with a gradual slope down to the Aliabad serai, which is about five miles distant and over a very easy road. On the left stands the octagonal tower, built of stone, pierced with loopholes and which is visible from so great a distance; there are also some huts, at one of which a draught of milk or water may usually be obtained. In clear weather the Minars at Lahore are visible, though at a distance of about 130 miles. The surrounding scenery is awfully grand, some of the adjoining peaks towering as much as 16,500 feet above the sea. The ALIABAD or BADSHAHI SERAI is one of the usual Mogul buildings standing alone in all its bleak and wild, yet grand and dreary solitude, high up the mountains, and buried in snow during the greater part of the year, when it remains unvisited by man. The *visitors' apartments* are inside the *serai*, and consist of a range of three good rooms on the side opposite its fine arched entrance; on the outside are some huts occupied, during the time the pass is open by *banyahs*, from whom the usual supplies may be obtained.

12. ALIABAD SERAI TO HIRPORE.—*Distance* 12*m.* *Time* 4½*h.*

Road continues down the valley, which gradually widens, and towards the end of the march opens into the plains of Kashmir; the first half is undulating, sometimes steep and rather rough, passes along the side of the mountains, and on the left bank of the roaring torrent which flows several hundred feet below; the latter half is nearly on a level with the river, and is easy both for walking and riding. *Lál Golám* is the name of a walled portion of the road about two miles from the *serai*; it is built out from the almost perpendicular side of the mountain, and overlooks a fearful precipice. Before this causeway was made many a dreadful accident happened at this place. Upon one occasion the path gave way as some elephants, conveying several of the ladies of the Emperor Aurungzebe's *zenána*, were going along it; some 14 or 15 of the former, and 3 or 4 of the latter, were killed, and probably before they even reached the bottom of the frightful precipice. A cannibal—*Lál Golam*—is said to have dwelt here, who killed the travellers by throwing them down the precipice, and afterwards devoured them at his leisure. To calm the timid, it may however be added that there is a grave a little above the road, and opposite a large pine tree, the reputed burial-place of this legendary monster. *Zujnar* is a watch-tower about a mile further on; *Shahkote* is an old fort on the right, across the river upon the edge of a plateau, and commanding the road up the valley; just after passing it the path descends to the *Suk-serai* an old building on the left bank of the *Rembiara*. Doobji is an encamping ground on the left bank of the river, and about three miles from Hirpoor; neither coolies nor supplies however are procurable, but there is a mineral spring a little way from it. HIRPOOR is a small and scattered village, prettily situated on the right bank of the *Rembiara* and in the middle of the valley, which is here about half a mile wide. The *visitors' apartments* form the left side of the interior of an old Mogul *serai* built in the time of *Akbar* at the southern end of the village, and consist of two upper rooms with stabling and accommodation for servants below.

13. HIRPOOR TO SHUPIYAN.—*Distance* 8*m*. *Time* 3*h*.

Road.—This is a short and easy march; the road continues along the right bank of the river; the valley gradually widens, and before going very far, the visitor obtains the first view of the Valley of Kashmir, and the lofty snow-clad mountains on its northern side. SHUPIYAN is the largest town on this side of the valley, and it is the commercial depôt for the Punjab. A short distance from it there is a very pretty wooden mosque, of which *Vigne* gives a very minute description, and which may be studied as a model of this type of Kashmirian building. There are two *bungalows*, and they contain ample accommodation.

14. SHUPIYAN TO RAMOO.—*Distance* 11*m.* *Time* 4*h.*

Road continues along the plains, and about three miles from Shupiyan it crosses the *Rembiara,* which flows in two or three branches which are bridged. About a mile further on it ascends the side of the low and densely-wooded hills in front, leads through the forest, past an old *zearut* or tomb on the right, and well worth examining, thence to *Shahjumarg*—an old *serai,* also on the right, and about seven miles from Shupiyan. About two miles further on it descends to the *Ramchú* river, which flows in several branches through a rich and narrow valley between two *kareewahs,* and after a mile or so it ascends its left side, and shortly leads to an old *dharmsala* or rest-house, which contains a room formerly available for visitors. RAMOO is about a mile further on; it is a considerable village on the left of the road, and situated under a low range of hills, the top of which commands an extensive view of the valley. The *bungalow* is on the right, opposite the village; it is double-storied, and contains four small rooms below and three larger above. The *zearut* of Sháh-núr-ú-din at Chrár can be visited from Rámoo, the journey to which from Hirpoor may easily be made in one day by breakfasting and changing coolies at Shupiyan. (*Vide Chapter IV.*)

15. RAMOO TO SRINAGAR.—*Distance* 18*m.* *Time* 6*h.*

Road is tolerably smooth and level all the way. There is an old *serai* at Khánpore, about six miles from Rámoo, containing a couple of rooms convenient for breakfasting. *Wahtor* is a pretty village with some very fine *chenar* trees about five miles further on, and is famous for its strong woollen socks and gloves. Thence to Srinagar the road is a made one, about 12 feet wide, and lined on both sides with poplars which were planted in 1864, and form a beautiful avenue. The *Rámbagh Serai* is a building on the left of the road, on the right bank of the *Dudhganga;* and the temple or *Chhatria* in the centre of the enclosure contains the ashes of His Highness the late *Maharajah Golab Singh.* Srinagar is the Capital of Kashmir, and is fully described in the following chapter. The *bungalows* for visitors are on the right bank of the Jhelam, and above the city; there are two ranges, the *upper* for married people, and the *lower*—that nearest the *Ameeri kadal*—for bachelors.

II.—GUJRAT AND PUNCH ROUTE.

This is an alternative route to that over the *Pir Panjàl* pass, and must be adopted when the latter is closed by snow, which, as previously stated, is usually from the end of October until the beginning of May. It branches off to the left of the *Pir Panjál* road about a mile beyond *Thana Mandi*, beyond which there are three passes—the *Rutten Pir,* the *Hắji Pir*, and that of *Baramoola.* The country lying between the two first belongs to *Moti Singh*, the Rajah of *Púnch*—a tributary of the Maharajah of Jamoo—and whose officials are also very attentive. This is the most difficult of all the authorized routes; the worst stages of it are those between *Kahoota* and *Ooree*, and that portion of the road from the top of the *Hắji Pir* to this last place is the worst of all. There are 18 stages, and they are as follows :—

List of Stages on the Gújrát and Púnch Route.

No.	Name.	Distance in miles.	Average time occupied exclusive of halting.
			Hours.
8	Gújrát to Thanna Mandi* ...	97½	...
9	Sooran ...	16	7
10	Púnch ...	14	6½
11	Kahoota ...	9	4
12	Aliabad ...	8	3½
13	Hydrabad ...	7	4½
14	Ooree ...	10	5
15	Naoshera ...	14	7
16	Báramúla ...	9	4
17	Patan ...	14	...
18	Srinagar ...	17	...

9. THANNA MANDI TO SOORAN.—*Distance* 16*m.* *Time* 7*h.*

Road.—About a mile beyond the bungalow, the Púnch road turns off to the left of the Pir Panjal road, and winding up the side of the hills on the left, it leaves the Thanna valley by a gap on the top of the ridge. After a slight descent, it ascends on the right, and leads through the forest to the *Rutten Pir Pass*, which is about six miles from *Thanna*, and the journey occupies about 2½ hours. The descent on the other side

* The stages from Gujrat to *Thanna Mandi* have been described in the previous route.

of the pass is easy; the road leads down a deep and very narrow gullee, covered with dense forest abounding with ferns; and the lower two-thirds of which are traversed by a small stream, which has to be forded about half a dozen times. This gullee opens into the valley of the *Sooran River*, which is here about 150 yards wide, and bounded on each side by rather lofty and usually sloping hills, covered with thick forest on the northern, and with grass upon the southern sides. Just after entering the valley the river has to be forded, and about a quarter of mile further on stands the village of *Bifliáj*, picturesquely situated on the side of the hill, about 400 feet above right bank of the river, and about three miles from the *Rutten Pir Pass.* From *Bifliáj* the road continues along the *Sooran* valley all the way, and is generally level and tolerably smooth; the first four miles are along the right bank of the river, and the path ascends the bank here and there when the river is high. About three miles from *Sooran* it crosses the river by a ford, and thence continues along its left bank. SOORAN is a small village, and contains a Thánna, in which a small military force is usually quartered. The BUNGALOW is situated a few hundred yards beyond it, and consists of a flat-roofed mud and stone building containing one room 12 feet square.

10. SOORAN TO PUNCH.—*Distance* 14*m.* *Time* 6½*h.*

Road continues along the *Sooran valley;* it crosses the river by a ford just opposite the village, and thence passes the whole way along its right bank. The first five or six miles pass over level turf covered with low jungle; the remaining eight through cornfields. Several springs may be seen along the roadside. About half-way a large stream has to be forded, which flows down from the mountains on the right, and along which a footpath leads up to *Gúlmarg,* four marches only from *Sooran.* PUNCH is a considerable town, containing about 500 flat-roofed houses, and situated in a wide and elevated plain surrounded by low and beautifully wooded hills. It is on the right bank of the *Sooran* or *Lair* River, which flows along its southern side and empties itself into the *Bitarh,* a large river which runs about a mile to the west of the town. The principal buildings are the palace, in which the *Rajah Motee Singh* usually resides; and the fort, which is a strong stone edifice, lately built. The bungalow is situated on the left bank of the *Bitarh,* about a mile beyond the town, and upon a pretty piece of greensward, under a *kareewah* or elevated table-land. It is a good substantial brick building with a flat roof, and contains two sitting-rooms, two bed-rooms, and two bath-rooms.

11. PUNCH TO KAHOOTA.—*Distance* 9*m.* *Time* 4*h.*

Road turns to the north and passes up the valley of the *Bitarh*, which is bounded by lofty and well-wooded hills, averages less than half a mile in width, and gradually narrows towards its upper end. The path re-ascends the high ground above the bungalow, and, after leading for a mile and half through cornfields, again descends to the river, and crosses a branch of it by a ford. After passing along its sandy bed for a mile and a quarter, it again crosses the stream by a ford, and re-ascends the left bank by a short but rather rough path, towards the village of *Diagwar*, which is about two miles further on, and about four miles from Punch. This village contains about 30 huts, situated upon an open and cultivated plain on the left bank of the *Bitarh;* there are some fine trees near it, which form a convenient and agreeable place for breakfast. A little way beyond it, and opposite *Chota Diagwar*, the path again descends to the river, and continues nearly on a level with it for about four miles, crossing and re-crossing it by fords about four or five times; about a mile and half from *Kahoota*, it leaves the level of the river, and ascends its right bank for about 300 feet, and thence continues with one intervening dip to the bungalow. KAHOOTA is a small village containing about 40 huts, and is prettily situated at the foot of the range of hills which bound a rich plateau, about 200 feet above the right bank of the *Bitarh.* The BUNGALOW is situated below the village and in the open fields, which are arranged in terraces; it consists of one room, with an enclosed verandah all round it.

As the supply of coolies and food at the next two stages is very uncertain, it is as well to make suitable arrangements before leaving Kahoota.

12. KAHOOTA TO ALIABAD.—*Distance* 8*m.* *Time* 3½*h.*

Road lies chiefly up a long and narrow valley, which leads to the foot of the *Háji Pir.* It passes by an easy ascent up to the summit of the spur which projects from the hills a few hundred yards beyond the bungalow, and then turns to the left and winds along the mountain side, where it is sometimes narrowed by the rocks on either side, and shortly descends to the very rocky bed of a stream which has to be forded. This stream is about three miles from *Kahoota*, and it flows into the *Bitarh*; the remainder of the road, which is occasionally very rough and sometimes steep, continues along its left bank all the way. On approaching *Aliabad*, the valley becomes much narrower, and the stream diminishes in size, but the hills increase in height, and assume the character of magnificent mountains whose sides, especially those on the left, are covered with forest. The *Hájí Pir* range closes its upper end, and the path leading over it may be seen from a considerable distance winding up its naked side. ALIABAD is a small village containing about 15 huts, built upon the side of the hill on the right. The BUNGALOW is a very rude structure, prettily situated in the midst of small green meadows, arranged in terraces, and about 200 yards below the village; it consists of one large room, and adjoining it are the ruins of an old serai.

13. ALIABAD TO HYDRABAD.—*Distance 7m. Time 4½h.*

Road.—In this march the *Háji Pir* range has to be crossed: the road is simply an ascent of about three or four miles on one side of the mountain, and a similar descent on the other. The ascent commences about half a mile from the bungalow, and is tolerably smooth, but rather steep in some places; and the mountain is bare of trees and exposed to the morning sun. There is a stone hut upon the top of the pass, which, during the hot weather, is occupied by a *fakir*, who is ever ready to administer a draught of milk or water, in exchange for a small present. The summit of the ridge, which is about 8,500 feet high, is covered with grass, and is tolerably level for about a quarter of a mile; the path then descends, becoming rougher and steeper as it proceeds, and in some parts it is a mere passage between the hard rocks. About a mile from the top, and about 20 yards from the right of the road, there is a spring, and just below it some broken pillars, probably portions of an old temple—the first ruins the visitor has yet met with. The path continues through dense forests all the way down to the bottom where a mountain torrent, which flows along a deep gorge on the left, has to be forded a few hundred yards from HYDRABAD. This is a very small village in Kashmir territory, and situated about half-way up the steep side of a very lofty range of mountains, which forms one side of a very deep and narrow valley traversed by the *Shah Kakuta*, a brawling and rapid torrent, formed by the junction of two streams which unite a few hundred yards above the village, from whence they may be seen rushing down their respective gorges. Supplies of food and coolies are very uncertain, and the latter should not be discharged until others are procured. There are two BUNGALOWS, both close to the village; the old one consists of two large rooms in the upper storey and the new one, three; abundant accomodation for horses and servants is attached to both of them.

14. HYDRABAD TO OOREE.—*Distance* 10*m*. *Time* 5*h*.

Road continues along the side of the valley, and on the left bank of the *Shah Kakuta* the whole way. This is the worst march along this route. On leaving the village, there is a gradual ascent for about a mile, then a gentle descent of about 300 feet to ford a mountain stream, then an ascent on the other side to a piece which is tolerably level for about half a mile; a long and steep descent then commences, which is often very rough, and sometimes narrow, and leads to the level of the river about three miles from *Hydrabad.* On nearing the bottom, a magnificent waterfall comes in sight, which, for height and volume, is one of the finest in *Kashmir.* After a few hundred yards the path again ascends to the left, and after several ups and downs, which, though short, are steep and rough, it leads to the village of *Talawari*, about six miles from *Hydrabad;* thence the road is tolerably smooth and level for about half a mile; it then ascends by a very steep, rough, and narrow path for about another half a mile, and then descends again by a similar road; after a tolerably easy quarter of a mile, a mountain stream is reached which has to be forded, thence the road passes chiefly through the fields, and finally joins the road from *Marri* near the bungalow. OOREE is a large village situated on the side of the hills to the left, and overlooks a beautiful amphitheatre about a mile and half in diameter, and bounded on every side by magnificent mountains. The River *Jhelam* flows along its northern side, rushing tumultuously through a deep and rocky gorge, with a roaring and hissing sound that may be heard from a long distance. An old stone fort stands upon its left bank, and near it, a little way up-stream, there is a very curious rope bridge well worth examining. The BUNGALOW is about half-way between the village and the fort; it is a new building and contains four large rooms, with four bath rooms placed at two of the corners.

III. RAWAL PINDI AND MARRI ROUTE.

This route is the most convenient for those residing at stations above *Jhelam* and it is usually open throughout the year. *Rawal Pindi.*—The starting point is a large civil and military cantonment on the *Grand Trunk Road*, about 169 miles above *Lahore*, with which it will ere long be in railway communication, and 101 below *Peshawar*; it contains a couple of good *Hotels*, besides an excellent *Dâk Bungalow*; there are several *European shops*, and *coolies*, *mules* and *ponies* are abundant. The *city*, which is rapidly increasing, was a place of note in the time of Alexander the Great, and the celebrated *Manikelya* tope, the reputed tomb of *Bucephalus* is only about 15 miles to the south-east of it. The number of stages in this route is 16; they are mostly short, and in fine weather any of them may easily be accomplished in one day, excepting those from *Hattian* to *Chakoti* and from *Chakoti* to *Oori*; they are as follows, viz:—

List of stages on the Rawul Pindi and Marri Route.

No.	Name	Distance in miles	Average time occupied exclusive of halting.
1	Rawal Pindi to Báratkao ...	13½	......
2	Trét	12	
3	Marri	14½	
4	Daywal	10	3½
5	Kóhála	10	3½
6	Chattar	10	4
7	Rára	9	3½
8	Tindáli	12	5
9	Gharri	9	4
10	Hattian	11	5
11	Chakoti	15	7
12	Oori	16	7½
13	Rámpore	11	4½
14	Báramula	13	5
15	Páttan	14	
16	Srinagar	17	

3. Rawal Pindi to Marri.—The distance is about 40 miles, and is usually accomplished in one journey, either by *dhooly dak* or by *Government hill cart.* The former is most convenient for ladies; the cost for each *dhooly*, including its return hire, is about 15 rupees, and the time occupied is about 12 hours or a night's journey. The latter is a light, low, and 2-wheeled covered cart,

drawn by two horses, and carries four persons, two in front, of which one is the driver, and two behind. The fare for one seat by the *ordinary* cart is about 10 rupees and by the *express* 16 rupees. The ordinary cart usually leaves the post-office early in the morning—the express at any time before 2 P.M., most convenient to the passengers; the time occupied by them both is about 4 or 5 hours. The road is metalled and fit for carriages all the way; the first 15 miles pass along the plains. There is a good dak *bungalow* at *Bárakao*, and also at *Tret.* and *Chattar* is about halfway, and there is a good *serai* belonging to *Sirdar Nihal Sing*, which contains a couple of rooms available for travellers: opposite it is a large Government garden. *Ghora Galli* is a small bazaar on the left, about seven miles below *Marri*, and beside it is a watch-tower, one of several built in the time of the *Rebellion* of 1857. The *Brewery*—an extensive range of buildings on the right—is about a couple of miles further on, lining the hillside, and just below and beyond it on the same side is the bridle path to *Marri*, which passes up by the *Lawrence Asylum*. *Sunny Bank*—the encamping ground—is alongside the carriage road three miles further on, and adjoins a good hotel. Marri* is a hill sanitarium and the summer seat of the Punjab

* *Vide* the "Marri Handbook, with Map and Key," by the Author.

Government; it contains about 150 houses, and a number of barracks forming a large military depôt; there is a club, three hotels, and several European shops, at which all kinds of articles suitable for the trip may be obtained. Applications for the supply of coolies and other carriage should be addressed to the Assistant Commissioner, in the event of any delay or difficulty arising with the *chowdris* appointed to supply them.

4. MARRI TO DAYWAL.—*Distance* 10*m.* *Time* 3½*h.*

Road is a steady descent nearly all the way, mostly through dense forest of oaks and pines, with an open spot only here and there, and is of an uniform width of 10 to 12 feet. Passing through the *Station*, it turns to the right of the *Post Office*, passes under the *Secretariat* and *Telegraph Offices* down to the *Flats* or *Cricket ground* 3 miles distant, then past the *Gharrial* ridge on the right and a little further on *Chumiari*, both hot weather encampments for British Troops. Thence it runs along the right side of the *Kanair* valley, which is deep, broad, and sloping, dotted with innumerable small villages, which are surrounded by fields, arranged in terraces. The scenery throughout is very beautiful. *The Bungalow* is situated near the village of *Hoseah*, and near some springs; it contains 4 sets of apartments, consisting each of a sitting, a bed, and bath room. There is a good *Serai* adjoining it. The view from the bungalow is particularly pretty, overlooking a triangular space bounded on the right by the Jhelam, and the Kashmir Mountains, and on the left by the Kanair stream and a lofty range which borders the Hazara District. Supplies and carriage of all kinds are abundant, and the arrangements good.

5. DAYWAL TO KOHALA.—*Distance* 10*m.* *Times* 3½*h.*

Road.—Open and exposed almost all the way, continues steadily descending down the *Kanair* valley until near the 6th mile, and a little beyond the village of *Béerot* when it suddenly turns to the right, and enters the valley of the *Jhelam,* now seen and heard rolling down its deep and rocky bed on the right and along which the whole of the remaining portion of this route continues as far as *Báramúla.* The last 2 miles are tolerably level, and a neat *suspension bridge* across the *Kanair* stream is passed within about 1½ miles of the bungalow. The scenery along this march, though less beautiful in its details, is grander than in the previous one; the pines, oaks and other large trees, as well as most of the English flowers and ferns being missing. The *Bungalow* is situated on a level plateau about 150 feet bove the road, and is exactly like that at *Daywal.*

This place consists only a few huts attached to the bungalow, the nearest village *Bakot* being some 2 miles distant; it is very hot and close from its confined position in the deep and narrow valley. Supplies and carriage are usually abundant.

It must here be noted that the old Road from *Kohala* to *Hattian*, across the *Danna* range, is not to be recommended; indeed it may be considered closed, for although there are old bungalows, no arrangements are now made for supplies or carriage; it is shorter, but steep and very rough; the stages are: *Danna*, 7½ miles; *Meira*, 8 miles; *Chikar*, 8 miles; and *Hattian*, 10 miles.

6. KOHALA TO CHATTAR.—*Distance* 10*m.* *Time* 4*h.*

Road.—This, like the previous march, is a hot one, as is indeed the case with all those between *Daywal* and *Hattian*, both inclusive. Immediately below and beyond the bungalow a fine *suspension bridge*, completed in 1871, and on which a small toll is charged, conducts the visitor into the territories of His Highness the Maharajah of *Jamoo* and *Kashmir*. The road now passes along the left bank of the river, and is of about the same width as before; there is a steady but easy ascent for the first mile or so; after that there is a series of ups and downs, mostly easy with here and there a level piece; the road frequently winds round the heads of small valleys or ravines, there passing over the rough beds of small mountain streams, in places cool and mostly shady. The road is open and exposed nearly all the way, except for a short distance within about a mile from the end of the stage. The scenery is everywhere grand; in several places the valley opens out, and here patches of cultivation, in terraced fields, are numerous and very pretty. CHATTAR is a small village on an open and cultivated plateau. The *bungalow*, about 150 feet above the river, is double storied, having four rooms below, with an open verandah all round, and two above with an open verandah in front of them; like all the others in *Kashmirian* territory it is rudely furnished with tables, chairs, and bedsteads; ordinary supplies and carriage, including riding ponies, are abundant, and there is a *khansamah* who is able to cook, and who has, at times, a small supply of beer, wine and spirits; this latter arrangement however is a recent one, is at present unlikely to succeed, and visitors are therefore recommended not to rely upon it.

7. CHATTAR TO RARA.—*Distance* 9*m.* *Time* 3½*h.*

Road.—This is an easy march but a hot one; immediately below the bungalow the road descends and passes over the unbridged stream, the *Agar* river, the same which had to be crossed between *Danna* and *Meira* on the old road; its bed is broad and very rough, and it is liable to be much swollen after rain, so as to delay the crossing for some hours,—a fact worthy of remembrance, especially by visitors hurrying back from leave. After crossing two other, but much smaller streams, the road continues up the valley of the *Jhelam*, and generally only a few feet above the river the whole way; it is for the most part straight, fairly smooth and level, the undulations being easy, the windings few, and most of the streams well bridged. Several waterfalls, two or three of which are very fine, may be seen, especially in the rainy season, on the mountains on the opposite side of the river. *Rára* is a very small village. The *bungalow* is prettily situated at about the same height above the *Jhelam*, and is of the same kind as that at *Chattar*, only that it has no upper storey; it is immediately opposite the gorge through which, with a loud and rushing sound, the milky waters of the *Nainsúk* from *Khaghán* emerge to join the *Jhelam*. The arrangements as to furniture, food, carriage and supplies, are the same as those at *Chattar*.

8. Rara to Tindali.—*Distance* 12*m*. *Time* 5*h*.

Road.—This is rather a long and somewhat fatiguing march; for the first three miles the road continues along the *Jhelam*, then it rises to the village of *Amon*, on the top of a flat, long, and cultivated spur, which runs down to a grand bend of the river; at the further end of this spur, the road turns abruptly to the right, and then descends to the bank of the river again; just opposite to this bend, which is about five miles from *Rara* the *Kishenganga* may be be seen joining the right bank of the *Jhelam*, with the town of *Mozufferabad* on its left bank, and on its right, in an open plain, are the ruins of an old *Mogul serai*. The descent to the river is about two miles, the remaining five are very undulating, passing mostly along the river bank, and at other times across cultivated fields; there is a very pretty waterfall in the latter part of the march; the *Abbottabad Road* may be seen running along the opposite bank of the river, which is now usually of a dark olive green colour; a Juniper fir and a willow, standing together, are seen on the edge of the opposite bank within about a mile and a half of *Tindáli*. The scenery throughout this march is grand, and after turning the bend above noticed the air becomes perceptibly fresher, the heat and oppressiveness experienced up to that point being less. The village of *Tindáli*, a very small one, is the residence of a Nawab, whose courtesy and attention to visitors deserve a word of warm acknowledgment. The *bungalow*, which is not seen until it is nearly reached, is situated on a low but open spot on the river's edge, and surrounded as it is by well-wooded mountains, with some fine rapids in the river immediately opposite, it is one of the prettiest spots along this route, especially when seen by moonlight. The accommodation in the bungalow, and the arrangements for carriage and supplies, are the same as those at the previous stage.

9. TINDALI TO GHARRI.—*Distance* 9 *m.* *Time.* 4*h.*

Road.—This is a short though rather rough march, there being several ups and downs, of which some, though short, are rather steep. Parties of navvies are at work levelling the road, which like all the other portions onwards towards *Báramula*, will in the course of time be made much easier than at present. The last two miles or so are mostly level, passing through the fields; the scenery becomes grander, and the number of English flowers and shrubs increases daily. GHARRI like *Tindali* is a very small village. The *bungalow* is situated in an open plain, a few feet only above the river; it is exactly like the previous one, and all the arrangements as to carriage and supplies are the same.

10. GHARRI TO HATTIAN.—*Distance* 11 *m.* *Time* 5*h.*

Road.—This is a pleasant and varied march, though it is exposed to the morning sun nearly all the way.

At first the road continues along the river for about a couple of miles, then there is a rather rough and tedious, though short ascent, with a similar descent; shortly after that a rough path leads up to a *col* or gap in the spur, which is seen in front jutting out from the hills, and projecting far into the valley causing a great sweep in the river which is now some distance from the road, and the sound of which is much missed. From this gap, which is about 4 miles from *Gharri,* the path descends into curious and pretty little plain, apparently once a lake, and now represented by a small *jheel,* full of reeds, lotus, &c.; after passing through this, on which there are some *chenars* or plain trees, the road turns sharply to the right, making a considerable detour to a very steep and narrow *khud,* in fact a "minor canon," the stream of which is bridged, and from which the ascent is very rough. It then leads over some terraced fields, and gently descending, it winds into another *khud,* where there are some rough but short ups and downs, soon after which it passes the old *Danna Road* on the wright, from hence the remaining two or three miles are, though hot, easy and very pleasant. From the junction of the *Kishenganga,* the bed of the *Jhelam,* thence called *Vedushtha,* becomes narrower and rougher, and the roaring and foaming of its waters gradually increase until near the *Báramula* pass, when it almost suddenly becomes broad, and as smooth and calm as a lake. HATTIAN consists of a few huts scattered high on the mountain side. The *bungalow,* visible long before it is reached, is situated on the opposite side of a wide mountain torrent, the rough bed of which is bridged in the ordinary simple fashion, that is, by long poles stretching from one bank to the other, and covered with planks, which are fastened at each end with wooden pegs. The *bungalow,* the entrance to which is overshadowed by a fine *chenar*, is on the same plan as that at *Gharri*, and the arrangements are in every respect the same. There are some fine pools in the adjoining stream, in which the angler may find some sport; he is warned however against the quality of the fish, which, as is the case indeed generally between *Kohala* and *Sopoor*, is very uncertain.

11. HATTIAN TO CHAKOTI.—*Distance* 15*m.* *Time* 7*h.*

Road.—This is a long and fatiguing march, for although it is generally tolerably smooth, there are several ups and downs, some of which are long, steep, and very rough, being in some places like high rocky steps, which are trying alike to the pedestrian and to the pony. On leaving the bungalow there is a steep and very rough ascent for about a quarter of a mile, after which the road is tolerably level for a mile or so, then there is a steep and very rough descent to a broad and bridged mountain torrent, with a similar but still rougher ascent on the other side, which renders this the worst dip upon the march. Thence there are easy undulations high on the grassy mountain side, through a forest of pine and oak, with a gentle descent to some terraced fields, on the edge of which, and about 6 miles from *Hattian*, there is a very fine *chenar* tree and a small clear stream near the villages of *Shirak* and *Saon*, a suitable place for breakfast, or for a short halt. Just beyond this, there is a short but rough descent and a similar ascent; then a mile or so level, smooth, and through shady forest to another steep, rough, and longer descent to a small unbridged stream, whence there is a long and steady ascent to a *dak ckoki*, situated on the top of the spur called *Koh Danda*, which is about half way and overlooks the plain and fort of *Kathai* on the opposite bank of the river. Thence there is a gentle descent down the very steep and grassy side of the mountains; the path is here about 1,000 feet above the river, and the mountains so steep that a stone set rolling does not stop until it reaches the river below; an officer's horse was killed here this year; moving too near the edge of the path, it somehow missed its footing, rolled about half way down the mountain side to a narrow ledge, where, after a few struggles it rolled down into the river, where it was at once lost sight of. A little further on there is another winding, rough, and steep descent to a bridged stream, on the other side of which is a similar ascent, after which the path is tolerably smooth and level for a mile or two. Then there is a long, steady, and in some parts rough descent to another bridged torrent, beyond which there is a similar ascent, and after passing through a fine forest, there is a gentle descent; after a short piece of level road, another, and the last rough, descent is reached, where there is a small cool stream just below the *bungalow* which now comes into sight, and is situated on the mountain side overlooking some extensive fields, which intervene between it and the river; it is upon the same plan as the last, and all arrangements for supplies and carriage are the same. CHAKOTI is a very small village.

12. CHAKOTI TO OORI.—*Distance* 16*m.* *Time* 7½*h.*

Road.—This is the longest and most fatiguing march along this route, but the scenery is everywhere very grand and in some parts even awfully so. A gentle walk from the bungalow leads to a rather rough and steep rise to the level of the fields, just beyond which there is a long but easy descent to a bridged mountain stream, falling in fine cascades down its narrow, deep, and rocky, yet wooded gorge, beyond which a rather steeper and rougher ascent leads again to the level, where, upon the left, may be seen a ruined *Mahomedan mosque*, beautifully carved in deodar wood, a good sample of those which will afterwards be very frequently met with in the *Kashmir valley*. After a mile or so, tolerably smooth and level, near a *dák choki*, there is another descent, winding, short, and rough, to a bridged stream, on the other side of which there is a very long and here and there very steep ascent, high up the pine clad mountain side, after which there is a tolerably smooth and easy descent with an occasional undulation to the village of *Haroosa*, which lies upon the terraced fields below. Just below this is the very wide and bridged *Haroosa Kuss*, the path down to which is tolerably easy, though the ascent on the other side is somewhat rough. After about half a mile of easy undulations the *Dardkot Kuss*, the widest as yet met, is reached ; the path down is pretty smooth but rather steep ; the stream at the bottom is bridged, and being about half way, and a cool and shady place, a halt for an hour or so, or for breakfast, is usually made here ; the ascent is much the same but to a higher point, which commands a good view of the very rocky gaps which here occur in the deep and narrow bed of the river. After an easy half mile or so, there is a short rough ascent, then a gentle smooth decline along the foot of the mountain richly covered with English flowers and shrubs, including the Hawthorn or May, to a couple of very old chenars at which there is another sharp descent, followed by a mile or so which is tolerably level; then after two or three more ups and downs, the path leads through some fields, on which the fort of *Oori*, about two miles distant, comes in sight. After passing some exceedingly old chenars on the right the descent to the *Oori Kuss*, the last and widest, begins; the ascent on the other side is still longer, steeper and more tedious, and it leads to the plain on which OORI stands. This is a small town consisting of a few houses, situated on the side of the hills, to the right, and overlooking a beautiful amphitheatre about a mile and a half in diameter, and bounded on every side by grand and lofty mountains. The *Jhelam* flows along its northern side and rushes tumultuously through a deep and rocky gorge, seething and foaming, magnificent to witness, with a roaring and rushing sound at times almost deafening, and which may be heard from a long distance. Near the old stone fort, on its left bank, and a little way up stream there is a very curious rope bridge, well worth examining. The *bungalow* is about half way between the town and the fort; it is upon the same plan as the previous one, and the arrangements for supplies and carriage are in all respects the same.

The GUJRAT AND PUNCH road joins the MARRI ROUTE at this place.

13. OORI to RAMPORE. *Distance* 11*m.* *Time* 4½*h.*

Road.—This is a comparatively easy march; the road passes mostly through shady shrubs and trees; the red and grey rocks hitherto met with are exchanged for a region of hard slaty strata, the scenery is grander than any yet seen. A few hundred yards across the plain the path leads to a long and rather steep and rough descent, to the bridged *Shah Kakuta*, the stream coming down from the *Punch Route*; then there is a similar ascent on the other side, and after a long and easy bend in a lateral valley, the road turns and descends once more into the *Jhelam* valley, on the opposite side of which, at this point, may be seen one of the old and ruined *Mogul serais.* The undulating path thence runs along the foot of the lofty pine-clad mountains, through dense shrubs and trees, at some distance above the river, the bed of which becomes narrower, and which now rushes along with a thundoring sound. After passing some lime kilns on the left, a large mass of rock is seen slightly above the level of the river, and under which, in a hollow, lives a blind *Fakir*. About half way, and, on the right, there is a very ancient ruin, covered with ivy, enclosed in dense forest, which is called *Pàndúghar;* it is an old temple consisting of an arched entrance, a central building inside, which is approached by a massive flight of steps, and the remains of an enclosing wall, besides many ruined masses, which lie scattered about the enclosure; it is probably one of the most ancient of its kind in or about *Kashmir,* and appears to have been built upon the same plan as the more famous ruins of *Martand* and *Awantipore.* The road shortly passes into a *Deodar* forest, and thence runs nearly on a level with the river, the second half of the march being generally smooth, tolerably level, and, like the first, shady, and very pretty. RAMPORE consists only of a very few huts, scattered about the forest. The *Bungalow* consists of a raised range of six sets of rooms, each containing a sitting room, dressing and bath room, with an open railed verandah running along its whole front; it is beautifully situated in an open space in the forest, and immediately opposite a lofty and almost perpendicular range of slaty mountains; like the others, it is partly furnished, and the arrangements for supplies and carriage are in all respects the same.

14. RAMPORE to BARAMULA. *Distance* 13*m.* *Time* 5*h.*

Road.—Though rather rough here and there, this is on the whole an easy and most delightful march, and conducts the visitor into the HAPPY VALLEY. The bridged *Harpat Kai* is crossed within a mile or so of the bungalow, and about a mile further on, and near *Bhaniar*, there is a fine old stone temple or *Mandir* in good preservation, a model of the ancient form, with central building, recesses on inner side of surrounding wall, and with the peculiar and characteristic trefoil arches; it is now used as a temple by Hindoos, with whom it is a favourite place of pilgrimage, and by whom a grand fair is held once a year. *Nowshera*, the old halting place, is about two miles further on ; there is a road to *Gulmarg* which leads up the gorge on the right from here ; it is said to be about 12 *koss* ; it is rather rough, and is reckoned two marches, the journey occupying about 8 hours. After many easy undulations and about five miles further on, the road drops into the pretty oval plain of *Kechama*, surrounded by low, well-wooded hills, and through which on the left, the *Jhelam* glides smoothly and calmly along, contrasting strikingly with its character in the previous march : at the further end of this plain, the path leads over the *Baramula pass* ; the ascent is steep but tolerably smooth, and occupies about a quarter of an hour ; the descent on the other side is also tolerably smooth, but is longer occupying about half an hour ; from the foot of the hills the road leads across the fields to the bank of the river, where there are two *Bungalows*, one exactly like that at *Rampore*, and the other smaller like those previously met with. The top of the *Baramula Pass* commands a fine view of a portion of the *Vale of Kashmir* including the *Jhelam*, the *Woolar Lake*, *Sopoor*, the snowy range of mountains enclosing it on all sides, and the *Takht-i-Suliman*.

Oh! to see it at sunset, when warm o'er the lake
Its splendour at parting a summer eve throws,
Like a bride full of blushes, when lingering to take
A last look of her mirror at night ere she goes!
When the shrines through the foliage are gleaming half shown,
And each hallows the hour by some rite of its own.
Here the music of prayer from a minaret swells,
Here the Magian his urn full of perfume is swinging
And here, at the altar, a zone of sweet bells,
Round the waist of some fair Indian dancer is ringing.
Or to see it by moonlight; when mellowly shines
The light o'er its palaces, gardens, and shrines;
When the waterfalls gleam like a quick fall of stars,
And the nightingale's hymn from the Isle of Chenars
Is broken by laughs and light echoes of feet
From the cool shining walks where the young people meet.
Or at morn, when the magic of daylight awakes
A new wonder each minute as slowly it breaks,
Hills, cupolas, fountains, called forth every one
Out of darkness, as they were just born of the sun.
When the spirit of fragrance is up with the day,
From his Harem of night, flowers stealing away;

And the wind, full of wantonness, woos like a lover
The young aspen trees till they tremble all over.
When the East is as warm as the light of first hopes,
And day with its banner of radiance unfurl'd,
Shines in through the mountainous portal that opes,
Sublime from that valley of bliss to the world.

BARAMULA.—The visitor is now fairly in *Kashmir Proper*, and the peculiarities of dress, language and features of the people—some of whom he will have met with on the previous march—as well as the construction of the houses, will at once strike him. *Báramúla* is a large town, situated on the right bank of the *Jhelam*, at the foot of a fine range of hills, and is a good sample of the Kashmirian towns generally; it contains about 800 houses, many of which are in a dilapidated state, and seem as though a breath of wind would bring them down; they are all built of *deodar* wood, and are mostly three or four storeys high, with pent roofs covered in with birch bark and overlaid with earth, which is usually clothed with grass and flowers. It was founded by *Hushki*, an Indo-Scythian Prince, and hence formerly called *Hushkipur*. There is a fine wooden bridge across the river, built in the same manner as all the others which span it in other parts of the valley; at its right end may be seen the ruins of a fine old *Mogul serai*, and at its left end is a *fort* of considerable strength; just above it on the left there is a fine *orchard*, and some distance below it on the same side there is a very sacred *zearat*, near which is a beautiful spring. *Gulmarg** may be visited from it. At *Ushkarah*, about a mile to the south-east of it, there is a Bhuddist temple, erected between A. D. 723 and 760, and discovered in 1865 by the *Rev G Cowie*, now Bishop of Auckland.

15 AND 16. BARAMULA TO PATTAN AND SRINAGAR.—The visitor has the option of proceeding from *Báramúla* to *Srinagar* either by land or by water. *By land* it is two marches—the first to *Pattan*, which is 14 miles, and the second, from *Pattan* to *Srinagar*, which is 17 miles: they are both very easy; the road is mostly level, and passes through lovely scenery all the way. *By water:* the visitor will scarcely hesitate to adopt this mode, for, after the fatigues of marching through the hills, the idea of travelling comfortably in a boat is too agreeable to be described. There are generally several *doongahs* at the *ghât* near the bungalows, and if the visitor has not already been waylaid on the road, he will quickly be surrounded on his arrival by boatmen, each praising the qualities of his craft, the strength and fastness of his crew, and supporting his statements by bundles of *chits* from his former employers. The business of engaging boats is sometimes very amusing and

* *Vide* Chapter V.

exciting, there is often great competition amongst the boatmen to secure a passenger, and not unfrequently the fascinations of the female members of the crew are brought to bear upon the undecided and to a susceptible bachelor—often with great and speedy success. The *doongah* is the ordinary passage boat, and the crew generally consists of four persons, male and female, whose fare is 8 annas each for the journey from *Báramúla* to *Srinagar*. One boat is sufficient for one person, including servants and baggage, but it is more convenient to engage a separate one for these, especially when the visitor is accompanied by his wife or family. The horses must be sent by land, as they cannot be conveyed in the boats.

The PASSAGE UP THE JHELAM occupies about 20 hours, and is a most delightful trip: the soft and balmy air —the broad, smooth, and glassy river—its verdant banks—the rich and cultivated fields—and, above all, those grand and snowy mountains, which entirely surround the beautiful valley, must be felt and seen to be fully appreciated. There need be no delay at *Báramúla*, for if a messenger be sent forward the day before, the boats may be in readiness on the arrival of the visitor and his baggage; and as soon as the *khansamah* has laid in a few supplies from the adjoining bazar, they may start at once, and the visitor can take his breakfast on the boat. This is towed up the river by a long line, pulled alike and in turn by the men and women, sometimes along one bank, and sometimes along the other; when the crew consists of four persons, two are usually engaged in towing, while the others sit in the boat, one steering with the paddle, and the other—usually one of the women—preparing the food, or occupied in some other domestic duty. These people live in their boats all the year round; they are their homes, and each contains at least one family, and usually several children—for they are a fruitful race.

DUBGAO is a small village on the right bank of the river, and about nine miles, or four hours' journey above *Báramúla;* there is a large timber depôt here, from whence most of the wood for boat-building throughout Kashmir is supplied; it belongs to the Government, and there are three or four bungalows in the fine grove of *chenars* near it, which are occupied by the agents attached to it. The *Pohra River* effects a junction with the *Jhelam* immediately above it; it is about two-thirds the width of the latter, and varies in depth according to the season of the year. It is one of the routes to the *Lolab*;* boats can usually ascend as far as the village of *Awatkúla* when the river is high, and the journey occupies about 20 hours. SOPOOR* is a town built

* *Vide* Chapter V.

upon both sides of the *Jhelam*, and is famous for *Mahseer* fishing; it is somewhat larger than *Baramúla*, from which it is about six hours' journey; the boatmen lay to here at evening, and start again early next morning. The WOOLAR LAKE* commences just above *Sopoor;* it is the largest in Kashmir, and the Jhelam flows through it; sudden squalls upon it are very frequent during the early part of the season, at which time the boatmen have a great and well-founded dread of passing through it. Goláb Singh was one afternoon overtaken by a storm upon it; he himself escaped with difficulty, but the 300 boats containing his attendants are said to have been all wrecked. When practicable, therefore, they soon leave it, and proceed by a canal which enters its southern side, and after winding through many miles of marshy ground, covered with reeds and lotus, swarming with mosquitoes, and studded with numerous villages, they re-enter the *Jhelam* by the *Noroo* Canal at *Shadipore.* In the later months, however, the boats must pass through the Woolar, and on reaching its eastern border the *Lanka Island* may be seen on the left; about a quarter of a mile beyond it there is a place called *Bánair*, a marshy portion of the left bank of the river, and opposite to which there is excellent fishing. The large village of *Hájan* is about three hours' journey

* *Vide* Chapter V.

beyond; in about four hours more the small village of *Súmbal* is reached, where there is a bridge; the mouth of the canal leading to the beautiful *Mánasbal Lake** is on the left, about a quarter of a mile below the *Súmbal* bridge. SHADIPORE,* about two hours' journey above *Súmbal*, is a very small village on the left bank of the *Jhelam*, and about six hours' journey from *Srinagar;* it signifies "the place of marriage," for here the *Sind* effects a junction with the right bank of the *Jhelam;* there is a Hindoo temple upon a solid block of masonry nearly in the middle of the river, overshadowed by a *chenar* which, tradition says, never grows. The CHOWNI, the site first selected by the late Maharajah *Golab Sing* for the visitors' bungalows, is on the left bank of the *Jhelam* and about a mile and half below *Srinagar;* there is a fine grove of poplars, and it is valuable for the encampment of visitors, but is too far from supplies and the city to be convenient.

SRINAGAR now comes in sight; it is built on both sides of the *Jhelam*, and if the water is low, the boatman paddle straight through it up to the *bungalows*, which are situated on its right bank, and a little beyond the city; if, however, the water is high, they find it easier to pass along the *Kut-i-kul* canal on the left bank, just above the last bridge or *Suffa kadal*, and the other end of which

* *Vide* Chapter V.

opens into the river near the Palace, and just below the *Ameeri kadal* or first of the seven city bridges. *Srinagar* is fully described in the following chapter; there are two ranges of *bungalows*—the *lower* for the bachelors, and the *upper* for married people; they are also described in the same chapter.

IV.—RAWAL PINDI AND ABBOTTABAD ROUTE.

That portion of this route from *Abbottabad* onwards was generally used by the Pathans, when Kashmir formed a portion of the *Dourání Empire,* and the road thither from *Cabul* lay *viá* the *Khyber Pass* to *Pesháwar,* and thence by *Hassan Abdal* and *Harripoor. Ráwal Pindi* is, however, the most convenient starting point for visitors. This route is not so much frequented as the previous one; the stages are much longer, and those six between *Mozufferabad* and *Báramúla* are greatly exposed to the noonday sun. In returning from Kashmir some visitors however, for the sake of variety, prefer it, as they do that of the *Gújrat* and *Púnch* route. The number of stages is 18, and they are as follows:—

List of Stages on the Ráwal Pindi and Abbottabad Route.

No.	Name.	Distance in miles.	Average time occupied, exclusive of halting.
	Rawal Pindi to		Hours.
3	Marri	40	
4	Khaira Galli	9	
5	Doonga Galli... ...	11	
6	Bára Galli	8	
7	Abbottabad	14	
8	Mânsera	13½	3½
9	Ghari	19	6
10	Mozufferabad ...	9	4½
11	Hattian	17	8
12	Kanda	11	5½
13	Kathai	12	6
14	Shâhdera	12	6
15	Gingle	14	7
16	Báramúla	18	8
17	Pattan	14	
18	Srinagar	17	

Rawal Pindi to Abbottabad.—The road and means of conveyance from *Ráwal Pindi* to *Marri* have been described in the previous route. From *Marri* to *Abbottabad* the distance is 42 miles; the road—smooth, wide, and mostly fit for carriages—lies through the mountains nearly all the way; the intermediate stages are three, as given in the list, but they are usually accomplished in one journey by *dhooly dâk,* a half of a few hours being made at Doonga Gullee, to afford the *kuhars* a rest, as they are not changed on the road, and 12 men are required for each dhooly; the cost is about 22 rupees, and the time occupied from 20 to 24 hours. The road is mostly fit for cantering; the scenery is particularly grand, and the *khuds* or precipices are often very steep; a pleasing variety of dense pine forests, grassy slopes covered with violets and other flowers, and deep gorges filled with glaciers, render the journey very enjoyable indeed in fine weather. There are several military encampments and permanent quarters along the roads—chiefly at the *gullees* as they are called, as Kyra, Changla, Doonga, Bara, and others; they are occupied during the hot season as *sanitaria* by detachments of European troops belonging to the Peshawar and Rawal Pindi Divisions.

ABBOTTABAD is a large civil and military station in the *Hazara* district—the head-quarters, in the hot season, of the *Commissioner* of Peshawar and of the *Brigadier-General* commanding the Panjab Frontier Force. It is a very pretty place, and entirely surrounded by low hills; its elevation is about 4,200 feet, and it is one of the healthiest and most desirable stations in the Panjab. It contains a good *Dâk bungalow*, some fair shops, and carriage and ordinary supplies are easily procured: beer, wines, and other such stores, however, had better be laid in at *Rawal Pindi* or *Marri*, if large quantities are required.

8. ABBOTTABAD TO MANSERA.—*Distance* $13\frac{1}{2}m$. *Time* $3\frac{1}{2}h$.

Road.—This is a very easy march along the plains, and the road is broad, level, and fit for carriages all the way. MANSERA is a considerable village built on both sides of the road, and on the left bank of a large stream, which is crossed by a substantial bridge. The BUNGALOW is situated on an eminence on the right of the road and above the village; there is a small and shady encamping ground just below it, on the left bank of the stream.

9. MANSERA TO GHARI.—*Distance* 19*m.* *Time* 6*h.*

Road.—This is also an easy march; the first half passes through the plains, and the road is exactly like that in the previous stage; the latter half leads through the mountains by a road which is smooth and undulating, and wide enough for the carriages of the Mountain Battery of Artillery, which moves out annually for practice from *Abbottabad* to *Ghari*. There is a pleasant place for breakfast in a fine clump of trees, on the left of the road, about nine miles from *Abbottabad*. GHARI is a large village situated on the left bank of the *Nainsuk*—a broad, rapid, and intensely cold river, which is crossed by a neat suspension bridge of wood and iron. The BUNGALOW is situated on the right bank of the river and just opposite the bridge. There is a small and shady encamping ground on the left bank of the river, behind the thannah.

10. GHARI TO MOZUFFERABAD.—*Distance* 9*m.* *Time* 5*h.*

Road.—This is a bad march; there is a range of hills to be crossed, and also a large river called the *Kishenganga.* The road is tolerably level for the first mile, and passes through the village; it then ascends to the *Doobballi* pass, which is about 3½ miles further on. The first mile and a half of the ascent is very steep, and occasionally rough, but the latter mile is tolerably smooth and level. The descent on the other side is about three miles long, and the path leads at first down the side, and afterwards along the bed, of a mountain torrent which flows through a narrow gorge, the lower end of which opens into the valley of the *Kishenganga.* The *ghat*, or landing place is about a quarter of a mile from the mouth of this gorge, the river is about 60 yards wide, very rapid, and is crossed by a rope bridge; there is also a good ferry boat, but it can only be used when the river is neither very high nor very rough. The fort on the left bank of the river was built by the *Pathans* to command the bridge and ferry. MOZUFFERABAD is about two miles from the ghât, and on the other side of a low range of hills which shuts it out from view. It is a small town built upon the hill side, and at a considerable height above the left bank of the *Kishenganga.* Supplies of food and coolies are abundant, and about half a dozen mules may usually be obtained. The BUNGALOW is about a quarter of a mile below the town, and is very pleasantly situated in a square enclosure a few feet above the left bank of the river; there is a convenient ghât for bathing below it, but the water is intensely cold.

11. MOZUFFERABAD TO HATTIAN.—*Distance* 17*m. Time* 8*h.*

Road.—This is a long and tedious march, in the first half of which there are three or four rather steep and rough places, but the remainder is tolerably level, although occasionally rough. The *Kishenganga* joins the right bank of the *Jhelam*—or *Vedusta* as it is called before its junction with that river—about a mile from *Mozufferabad;* from thence the road continues along the right bank of the latter river nearly the whole way to Báramùla, and parallel to the Rawalpindi and Marri road, which may be seen on the opposite side of the river. HATTIAN is a small village at the foot of the mountains, and is not visible until it is nearly reached; the river may be crossed by a rope bridge just opposite to it. The BUNGALOW is situated on the further side of the village, a few feet above the river, and resembles that at *Mozufferabad.* The water in the river is warmer than that of the *Nainsúk* and the *Kishenganga.*

12. HATTIAN TO KANDA.—*Distance* 11*m.* *Time* 5½*h.*

Road.—This is a fair march; the road is very undulating; but the ups and downs, although mostly rough, are not usually steep. About three or four miles from *Hattian* there is a very steep and rough descent to a stream, and there are two or three others within about four miles of KANDA, which is a very small village on the side of a ravine, a little to the left of the road. The BUNGALOW is situated about 50 feet above the river, and is double-storied.

13. KANDA TO KATHAI.—*Distance* 12*m.* *Time* 6*h.*

Road.—This is a rough march, containing two or three rather steep places, one about four miles, and another about eight miles from *Kanda;* they lead down to mountain streams which are bridged. KATHAI is a small village situated in the middle of a wide and open plateau high above the river; there is a mud fort just beyond it. The BUNGALOW is situated on this side of the village, and resembles that at Hattian.

14. KATHAI TO SHAHDERA.—*Distance* 12*m.* *Time* 6*h.*

Road.—This is also a rough march, and resembles the previous one; near the fourth mile there is a fine waterfall, and between the sixth and ninth miles there are three or four deep ravines, where the road is rather steep and rough. SHAHDERA is a very small village upon a plateau like that at *Kathai.* The BUNGALOW is double-storied, each containing three rooms, and the upper one is reached by stairs from one of the lower rooms.

15. SHAHDERA TO GINGLE.—*Distance* 14*m.* *Time* 7*h.*

Road.—This is a good march; there are three or four dips in the first half, but they are neither rough nor steep; and the other half of the road is mostly smooth and level. There is a ruined *serai* on the right, about half-way; and adjoining it is a small enclosed orchard —a convenient place for breakfast: it contains a very old wooden shrine or *zeárat,* built in the peculiar Kashmirian style, and well worth examining. *Ooree* is visible on the opposite bank of the river, just before reaching this *serái,* and a rope bridge may be seen crossing the river just beyond the fort. GINGLE is a small village situated in a small, open, and cultivated plain above the river; the valley is very narrow here, but the mountain scenery is very magnificent. The BUNGALOW is built near the bank of the river, and is double-storied; each story contains three rooms with an open verandah along the front, and the upper one is reached by stairs from the lower verandah.

16. GINGLE TO BARAMULA.—*Distance* 18*m.* *Time* 8*h.*

Road.—This is a long march, but easy and pretty; for the first 13 miles the road is smooth and tolerably level, and continues along the bank of the river; it then ascends the range of hills on the left, and leads through a short and narrow pass, at the further end of which the visitor will obtain the first glimpse of the *Vale of Kashmir.* Descending to the plains, the road leads again to the right bank of the now wide, smooth, and beautiful *Jhelam,* and conducts to the town of BARAMULA, which has been already described in Route No. iii.—*The Rawal Pindi and Marri*—in which will also be found the continuation of this route to *Srinagar.*

CHAPTER III.

CITY OF SRINAGAR.

Population and houses—Public and private buildings—Jhelam—City bridges and canals—Jhelam embankment and ghàts—Visitor's bungalows—Conditions of occupation—Emcamping grounds—The Baboo—Civil officer on duty—The Chaplain, and Cemetery—The Doctor on duty—Drinking Water—Native tradesmen—Down the river—The Dal, or City Lake.

SRINAGAR* or *Suryea Nagar*, the City of the Sun, built by Rajah *Pravarasene* about the beginning of the 6th century, is the Capital of Kashmir, and a plan of it will be found in Montgomerie's *Jamoo and Kashmir Map.* It is situated about midway between the two ends of the valley, and close to the hills which bound its north-western side; it is built upon both sides of the *Jhelam*, and extends along its banks for about two miles; its elevation is about 5,276 feet above the sea, but it is almost surrounded by low swampy tracts, which render it unhealthy. Its population is estimated at 150,000

* A beautiful series of photographic views of the City, and many other portions of *Kashmir* has been taken by *Bourne and Shepherd* of Simla and Calcutta, and by *Baker and Burke* of *Marri* and Peshawur, both of which Firms have courteously offered copies of them for an illustrated edition of this *Guide*, the publication of which may hereafter be undertaken in London.

souls, of whom 20,000 are *Hindoos*, and the remainder *Mahomedans*. It contains about 20,000 houses, which are mostly built of wood, and are generally three or four stories high, with pent roofs overlaid with earth, which, during the greater part of the year, is clothed with grass and other plants; owing to their inflammable nature fires are very frequent, and sometimes, especially during the hot and dry season, very extensive. It also contains two Royal Residencies for the use of the Maharajah, during his usual summer stay in Kashmir, for it may here be mentioned again that *Jamoo* is the ancient and original, province of the family of the Maharajah who are *Rájpúts* of the highest caste, and of the tribe called *Dogras*. Kashmir as well as the surrounding countries of *Ladák*, *Gilghit*, *Astor*, *Iskardo* and others, being comparatively recent acquisitions to the dominions of this now powerful and extensive sovereignty.

The PUBLIC BUILDINGS are but few; the principal of them are the *barah-darri*, *palace*, *fort*, *gun factory*, *dispensary*, *school*, and the *mint*; also some ancient *mosques*, *temples* and *cemeteries*, which the student of Kashmirian history may study with advantage. The *streets* are generally narrow, and some of them are paved with large and irregular masses of limestone; they are all however very dirty and unfit to be visited by ladies.

There are several *bazars* or market-places in different parts of the city, one of which called the *Maharàj Gange*, has been lately built for the convenience of visitors, in which all the manufactures peculiar to Kashmir may be readily obtained. There are several large *mansions* on its outskirts, which are chiefly occupied by the great shawl merchants and bankers; some of them exhibit beautiful specimens of trellised wood-work, and in other respects are very tastefully fitted up.

The River Jhelam divides the city into two nearly equal portions, which are united by seven bridges, the names of which, enumerated from above, are—the *Ameeri Kadal*, the *Hubba Kadal*, the *Fati Kadal*, the *Zaina Kadal*, the *Allee Kadal*, the *Naya Kadal*, and the *Saffa Kadal.* The average breadth of the river, as it flows through the city, is about 88 yards; its depth is variable, but the average during the season is about 18 feet. Its sides were formerly embanked from the first to the last bridge; some portions of this embankment are still perfect, but others have been entirely washed away, or otherwise removed, whilst others are now tottering, and seem ready to fall at the slightest touch. This Jhelam embankment was a work of art, composed chiefly of long rectangular block of limestone, and most of them of very large dimensions; amongst those remaining many blocks of carved stones are seen, which are portions of some of those fine ancient temples, the ruins of which lie scattered all over the valley. There are several very fine stone *ghâts* or landing stairs, leading down to the river. The city is also intersected by several canals, the principal of which are the *Sunt-i-kul* the *Kut-i-kul*, and the *Nálli Már.*

The BUNGALOWS FOR VISITORS are all situated above the city; they are built in orchards, are all upon the right bank of the river, and in two separate ranges. The lower one, which commences about 400 yards above the first bridge, or *Ameeri Kadal*, is intended for bachelors; the upper one, commencing about a quarter of a mile above the lower range, is for married families.

The *bachelor range* contains about four bungalows, standing in three orchards, which beginning from below, are named the *Tára Singh Bágh Gurmuk Singh Bágh*, and *Harri Singh Bágh.*

The *married range* is built in the *Moonshi Bágh*, and consists of about 16 detached bungalows; and three separate and raised terraces, each containing six sets of quarters of three rooms in each.

They are all partly furnished and are rent-free, His Highness the Maharajah having generously declined the suggestion of the Indian Government that visitors should pay for occupying them; he however reserves to himself the right of resuming or retaining either or any of them which he may require for the use of special visitors.

The POST OFFICE is situated in the lower, or bachelor range of bungalows.

On ARRIVAL AT SRINAGAR it is advisable to communicate as early as possible with the *Native Agent*, *Baboo Amarnath*, who is deputed by the Maharajah to attend to the varied wants of European visitors. His office is near the river end of the *poplar avenue;* it is known as the *Baboo-ke-dafter*, and is usually open until 5 or 6 o'clock in the evening. He generally attends daily at the bungalows or tents of the visitors to receive orders, or to afford assistance or information. Police arrangements are also under his control, although he possesses no magisterial authority. He is the highest authority upon all points connected with the prices of articles, rates and fares, and like subjects; the following copy of the LOCAL RULES demands the most careful attention of all visitors:—

Local Rules for the guidance of Visitors in Kashmir, published under the sanction of the Punjab Government.

1. VISITORS wishing to visit the Fort and Palace are required to give notice of their intention on the previous day to the Babu deputed to attend on European visitors.

2. Visitors about to proceed into the interior, and wishing to be supplied with carriage, are requested to communicate with the Babu as least 30 hours before the time fixed for their departure. Failing this notice the Babu cannot be responsible for the supply of carriage in proper time.

3. Cows and Bullocks are under no circumstances to be slain in the territories of his Highness the Maharaja.

4. Visitors are not permitted to take up their abode in the town, in the Dilawar Khan Bagh, or in the gardens on the Dal Lake, *viz.*, the Nishat and Shalimar gardens, and the Chashma Shahi. The Nasim Bagh is available for camping. The fixed camping places in Srinagar are as follows,—the Ram Munshi, Munshi, Hari Singh, and Chenar Baghs.

5. Servants of visitors found in the city after dark, and any servant found without a light after the evening gun has fired, will be liable to be apprehended by the police.

6. Servants of visitors found resorting for purposes of nature to places other than the fixed latrines will be liable to punishment.

7. Grass-cutters are prohibited from cutting grass in or in the neighbourhood of the gardens occupied by European visitors.

8. All boats are to be moored on the left bank of the river, and no boatmen are allowed to remain at night on the right bank.

9. When the Dal gate is closed no attempt should be made to remove the barrier or to lift boats over the *bund* to or from the lake.

10. Visitors are not permitted to shoot in the tract of country extending along the lake from the Takht-i-Suliman to the Shalimar gardens, which is a preserve of His Highness the Maharaja; shooting on the tracts marginally noted, which are private property, is also prohibited.

Doputta.
Kukaiwalla.
Machipura.
Danna Chikar.
Qori.
Bunyar.

11. Visitors are prohibited from shooting the heron in Kashmir.

12. Fishing is prohibited at the places marginally noted, as also between the 1st and 3rd bridge in Srinagar.

Martand.
Verneg.
Anantnag.
Devi Khirpowani.

13. Houses have been built by His Highness the Maharaja for the accommodation of visitors—those in the Munshi Bagh being set aside for the use of married people, and those in the Hari Singh Bagh for bachelors. With the exception of the houses reserved by His Highness for the private guests, and those reserved for

the Civil Surgeon, dispensary, and library, all the houses are available for visitors and are allotted by the Babu.

14. Married visitors are allowed to leave the houses occupied by them for a term of seven days without being required permanently to vacate the same. After the expiration of that period the Babu is empowered to make over the premises to another visitor requiring house accommodation ; any property left by the former occupant being liable to removal at the owner's risk. Bachelors are allowed to leave their houses for a period of three days subject to the same conditions.

15. Visitors are required to conform strictly with all local laws and usages.

16. In all matters where they may require redress, and especially on the occurrence of robberies, visitors are informed that they should refer, as soon as practicable, to the Officer on Special Duty.

17. Visitors are particularly requested to be careful that their servants do not import into, or export from, the valley articles for sale on which duty is leviable. The baggage of visitors is not examined by the Maharaja's Customs officials, and in return for this courtesy it is expected that any evasion of the Customs Regulations will be discountenanced.

Tariff of boat hire.

THE hire of a doonga with crew is Government Rs. 15 per mensem. The crew should consist of at least four persons; women and children over 12 years of age to be considered as able-bodied members of a crew.

The hire of a shikarah is determined by the number of the crew, who are paid at the rate of Government Rs. 3 per mensem and annas 8 for the boat. When boats are taken out of Srinagar, boatmen are entitled to *rassad* at the rate of half an anna per man per diem.

Tariff of doonga hire by distance.

From Baramula	to Srinagar,	per boatman	...	0	8	0
Do. Srinagar	to Baramula,	ditto	...	0	6	0
Do. do.	to Islamabad,	ditto	...	0	8	0
Do. Islamabad	to Srinagar,	ditto	...	0	6	0
Do. Srinagar	to Awantipur,	ditto	...	0	6	0
Do. do.	to Manasbal,	for the trip	...	1	0	0
Do. do.	to Ganderbal,	ditto	...	1	2	0
Do. do.	to Awatkula,	ditto	...	3	0	0

When boats are ordered from Srinagar to meet a visitor at any place, half hire of the boat from Srinagar is payable in addition to the fare to the place whence the visitor is proceeding. When a boat is not used on the date for which it is ordered, annas 8 per diem is payable for detention."

Three EUROPEAN OFFICERS are deputed every season by the Indian Government for duty in Kashmir—a *civil officer*, a *chaplain*, and a *medical officer*—to each of whom a special residence in Srinagar is assigned by the Kashmirian Government; they usually, however, pass the months of July and August at *Gulmarg* or *Sonamarg*.

The CIVIL OFFICER ON SPECIAL DUTY lives in the Residency—a large bungalow between the married and bachelors' bungalows on the right bank of the river; he is the medium of communication between the visitors and the Kashmiri officials; he is invested with the full powers of a Sessions Magistrate; all British subjects are amenable to his jurisdiction, and in cases of gross misconduct he may summarily order any one of them to quit the Maharajah's dominions. It is customary for officers to call, or leave their cards, upon him.

The CHAPLAIN on duty performs divine service every Sunday at the old Residency in the *Shaikh Bagh* which also contains the European Cemetery.

THE MEDICAL OFFICER on duty is deputed to attend upon the European visitors in Kashmir, and his usual residence is in Srinagar. A *medical missionary* in connection with the Church Missionary Society is also stationed there during the season. It may here be added that the climate of *Srinagar* is generally very malarious and unhealthy in July and August, and visitors are therefore recommended to spend those months at *Gulmarg*, *Sonamarg*, in the *Lolab*, or in some other elevated locality: the benefit of moving only two or three miles from the vicinity of the city is then often as sudden as it is surprising.

DRINKING WATER should not be taken from the *Jhelam*, but from a fine spring at the foot of the *Takht-i-Suliman* hill and a little to the back of the *Moonshi Bagh;* the purest of all, however, is that from the *Chashma Shahi*, which is situated on the south-eastern side of the *Dal* or city lake, and from which the *Royal Palace* is daily supplied.

Before the visitor is fairly settled in Srinagar, he will be besieged by the various classes of TRADESMEN, artisans, and others,* soliciting orders or employment. The following are the principal of them, *viz.*:—

	OCCUPATION.
1	Shawl Merchants and Woollen Drapers.
2	Clothiers and Tailors.
3	Gold, silver and copper-smiths.
4	Papier-mache Makers.
5	Leather Workers.
6	Precious Stone Dealers.
7	Boatmen.
8	Shikarees.
9	Basket, Makers.

* *Vide* Appendix No. 2.

The Kashmirian tradesmen have no fixed rates of prices, but, following the custom equally prevalent throughout India, they usually regulate their demands according to their estimate of the income or *talab* of each customer; their prices have much increased of late years, and the quality of their work deteriorated, indeed they are very prone to *scamp* it, in some cases perhaps from a profusion of orders, but they usually require strict supervision. In cases of disputes, the Baboo is recommended as the final referee.

The POPLAR AVENUE is the *Rotten Row* of Srinagar, and is just behind the *Moonshi Bagh;* it commences near the *Ameeri Kadal*, behind the *Shaikh Bagh*, and terminates near the end of the *Sunt-i-kul* or apple-tree canal, opposite that bare and rocky hill at the foot of the *Takht-i-Suliman.* It was planted by the Sikhs, is quite straight, about a mile and one-eighth long, and fifty-six feet in average width, and in 1865 it contained in all 1,714 trees, of which 1,699 were *poplars* and 15 *chenars.*

The visitor is recommended to take a GENERAL VIEW of the city and its neighbourhood, from the top of the *Takht-i-Suliman*, and the *Harri Parbat* or fort hill, before examining the various places in detail.

The TAKHT-I-SULIMAN, or *Throne of Solomon*, is the hill behind the married range of bungalows; its elevation is 6,263 feet above the sea, or about 1,038 feet above the level of Srinagar. There are two roads to the top of it; the easier one is that upon its western side, which commences behind the village of *Drogjun*, a few hundred yards from the gate of the *Dal* or city lake called the *Dal-ke-darwaza*, and which may be reached either by land—which is the quickest, or by water; this path was made by the Maharajah *Golab Singh* a short time before his death, and is composed of wide stone steps extending nearly all the way up; the ascent occupies from 30 to 40 minutes, and even ladies have ridden on horseback to within a few yards of the top, but it is safer for them to ascend in *dondies* or *jampans* backwards: gentlemen ascend on foot; at the end of the first third there is a level piece about 50 yards long, and another at the end of the second third about 70 yards; the steepest portions are the first 100 yards, and the last 20. The other path is on the eastern side of the hill, and is very rough, although not very steep; it is only fit for practised walkers. Upon the top of the hill, which is of trap, there is a fine old STONE TEMPLE, which the Hindoos call *Shankar Accharya;* it was originally *Bhuddist,* but in later times was turned into a *mosque;* it was erected by *Jaloka,* son of *Asoka,* who reigned about 220 B.C. It is raised upon an octagonal base of solid masonry, upon the eastern side of which are stone steps leading up to it; the first 12 steps conduct to a small archway, which is 22 inches wide and 6½ feet high, and closed by a pair of wooden doors. Within this archway there is a fine flight of 18 polished lime-stone steps, which are bounded on each side by a solid balustrade of the same material, about 6½ feet high; the steps are each 8 feet wide, 1 foot high, and 1 foot broad, and they lead to the top of the octagonal base which supports the temple. There is a stone pavement round the outside of the temple, 9 feet wide, and bounded by the remains of an elaborate stone parapet 4¼ feet high. The temple itself appears much older than the flight of steps leading to it; its interior is circular, 14 feet in diameter, and its roof is flat and 11 feet high; the walls are covered with white plaister composed of *gypsum*, and the roof is supported upon four octagonal limestone pillars. In the centre of the floor is a quadrangular stone platform, 1 foot high, 5¾ feet long, and 5¼ feet broad; it supports a *lingam* or idol of black stone, around which is carved a coiled serpent; the *lingam* is 18 inches high, 2½ feet in circumference, and it stands in the middle of the *yoni*. Upon the hinder of the two pillars on the left there are two Persian inscriptions; that upon the front of it states that this *bút* or idol was made by *Raji Hashti*, a *sonár*, in the year 54 of the *Samat* or Hindoo era, or about 1,870 years ago; while that at the foot of the back part of the same pillar states that "he who raised up this idol was *Kwájah Rokm*, son of *Mirján*, in the year——:" the remainder of the inscription is below the pavement, and cannot be made out. Besides the temple, there are also ruins of other buildings on the top of the hill; on the northern side is a square flat-roofed room entirely built of stone, and on the south-west another small ruin. The view from the platform surrounding the temple is grand, and well repays the exertion of ascending the hill; it commands nearly the whole length and breadth of the valley, and presents a complete panorama of the *City Lake*, the *Peri Mahal* or Fairy Palace, the *Harri Parbat* or Fort Hill, the *City*, the *Apple-Tree Canal*, the *Poplar Avenue*, and the *Jhelum*, which is perhaps the most beautiful portion of the whole scene, on account of its series of curves, which are said to have suggested the peculiar pattern of the shawls.

THE HARRI PARBAT OR KOHI MAHRAN is an isolated hill, about 250 feet high, and surmounted by the Fort; it stands on the northern outskirts of the city, and is about 2½ miles by land from the lower range of bungalows. The road to it lies along the *Poplar Avenue*, and over the bridge at its upper end, which crosses the *Suntikul* Canal; then to the left through the village of *Drogjun*, over the bridge at the *Dul-ke-Darwaza*, or gate of the City Lake, and thence along an ancient causeway which divides the lake from the canal, and which is lined with poplars; after passing a few hundred yards towards the right, it leads to a high bridge across the *Mar Canal*, which flows from the lake and intersects the northern half of the city; about 30 yards beyond, it turns sharp to the right, shortly leads into an open space, from whence the fort is visible, and taking a northerly direction, conducts to the principal gateway in the wall surrounding the hill, which is called the *Kátí Darwáza*, over which there is a Persian inscription giving the date and other particulars of its construction. The stone wall, as well as the fort, was built by the Emperor *Akbar* about A.D. 1590, and at a cost of about a crore of rupees, or £1,000,000 sterling; its length is about 3 miles; it is 28 feet high, 13 feet thick, and is strengthened at intervals of about 50 yards by bastions, which are about 34 feet high, and loopholed, like the upper part of the wall. At present there are but three gateways—the *Káti Darwaza* on the south-east, the *Bachi* on the west, and the *Sung-heen* on the north-west, where *Akbar* designed a new city (*Nagar*); there is not a living soul there now, and blocks of stone, brought from the ancient temples of Kashmir, lie in desolate grandeur all around.

The *fort* occupies the summit of the hill, and was built by *Akbar* to overawe the capital which had just before revolted; it is of stone, and consists of two wings placed nearly at right angles to each other, and a separate square building, with a bastion at each end, situated just below the western wing. It may be reached by two roads, one beginning at the northern side of the hill, which is broad, easy, and fit for riding, and the other commencing at the foot of its southern face, which is steep and rugged. From a distance the fort presents a formidable appearance, but its interior is very disappointing; it contains only a few wretched huts, used as barracks by the small garrison, a couple of tanks filled with slimy water, and a small Hindoo temple; the bastio ns, hoever, contain about three guns each, which are worthy of inspection on account of their age and peculiar construction. *Zeman Shah*, the Afghan *Shah Suja*, was for some time imprisoned in it.

The view from the top of the *Harri Parbat* is very fine; the city, spread out on the south, resembles a green carpet, for the roofs of the houses are clothed with grass and other plants, and by the aid of a pair of binoculars every building of interest may be easily distinguished. The *Takht-i-Suliman* stands out boldly and distinctly on the south-east, while on the east lies the *Dal* or City Lake, which is here seen to the best advantage; on the southern side of the hill is a very fine old ruin, called the *Akhun Mullah Shah Masjid*, after the tutor or spiritual guide of the Emperor *Jehan Gir;* to the west of this is the shrine of *Shah Hamza*, otherwise *Makdum Sahib*, which is of great sanctity among the Mahomedans; and on the northern side of the hill is a large and irregular *mass of rock*, which has been dedicated by the Hindoos to *Vishnu;* it is covered with red pigment, and is much frequented by the Hindoo community as a place of worship.

Down the River.

Two or three days may well be spent in visiting the various places of interest upon or near the banks of the river; for this purpose a small boat or *shikarah* is necessary, and the following table will be found useful by enabling visitors to regulate their movements:—

Time Table for Journeys in Shikarah with a crew of six men.

Time occupied.	From To	To From	Time occupied.
20 minutes ...	Moonshi Bagh	Shaikh Bágh Ghat ...	12 minutes
30 do. ...	Ditto ...	Sher Garhi ...	20 do.
1 hour ...	Ditto ...	Sháh Hamadán Masjid	35 do.
1¼ hour ...	Ditto ...	Saffa Kadal ...	45 do.
20 minutes ...	Ditto ...	Ram Moonshi Bágh..	30 do.
30 do. ...	Ditto ...	Vathnár Nalli ...	45 do.

The SHAIKH BAGH is an enclosed orchard below the *bachelors' range* of bungalows: it contains the old Residency, now used as a *church*, and the *European Cemetery*. The latter is situated at the southern corner of the garden, and to the left on entering from the *ghât*; it is enclosed by a wooden railing, was consecrated in May 1865 by the Bishop of Calcutta, and it then contained 14 graves, but the number is now increased to 25.* On the death of a visitor the Maharajah sometimes presents a shawl to wrap the body in.

The BARAH DARRI, a new and beautiful royal pavilion, lately built for the use of the Maharajah or any of his distinguished guests, is opposite the *Shaikh Bagh Ghat*; the doors and ceilings are of *Papier Maché*, the walls tastefully painted in scroll work, and in each room there is a large chandelier of fine cut glass; there is also a smaller pavilion at each end of the raised terrace upon which it stands, and which is reached by a noble flight of stone steps.

* Mr Robert Thorp, at one time a Lieutenant in the 89th Regiment, and who afterwards wrote a pamphlet inveighing against the Kashmir Government, is buried here; he expired suddenly one morning in November 1868, at Srinagar, after ascending the *Takht-i-suliman*; the cause of death was rupture of the heart, as was proved by a *post mortem* examination. At the request of the Kashmir Government a Commission of Enquiry, composed of *Mr. R. T. Burney* of the Civil Service and the *Author* was deputed to proceed to Srinagar, to investigate the circumstances of his death, but at the moment of their starting from Marri they received intimation from the Panjab Government that *Surgeon H. Caley*, while on his way from Ladak, had examined the body, and furnished his report to the above effect; the departure of the Commission was therefore counter-ordered.

The CITY DISPENSARY is just below the *Barah Darri;* it is one of several now established in various parts of the Maharajah's territories, and the daily number of the out-patients averages between 150 and 200; there is also accommodation for about 50 in-patients; the stock of European medicines is usually abundant, and the quality very good; a vaccinator is attached to it, besides a British Hospital Assistant and a large staff of subordinates, who are all under the superintendence of a fully qualified Bengal Assistant Surgeon, whose salary is 500 British rupees a month, and who is also Physician to the Royal household. These institutions are very popular, and most creditable to the Kashmir Government.

The PARADE-KI-GHAT is between the *Barah Darri* and the *Dispensary;* it leads to the smaller *parade ground* where the Maharajah gives his afternoon parties, and where the visitors enjoy the games of cricket, badminton, and also *polo*, which has now become so fashionable at home, and which has been imported from Little Tibet, where it is called *Chogan*, and of which an illustration may be seen in *Vigne's Travels;* it is often played by the natives on this parade ground. The *Hazari Bàgh* is a garden on the left side of the parade ground; it has been made by the present Maharajah, and is well worth visiting. The *Ràm Bàgh* contains the tomb, *chhutri* or *suma d*, of Golab Singh, and should be visited; it is on the Shupiyan road, about a mile beyond this parade ground, and upon the bank of the *Dudh Ganga* river; a new *serai* for Hindoo Pilgrims and other travellers is built around it. The *gun factory* is about ten minutes' walk from the *parade-ke-ghat*, and straight across the parade ground; it is worth visiting, but an order from the Baboo is necessary. The *grand parade ground* is about ten minutes' walk to the south-west of the gun factory, and on the other side of the bridge at the end of a long and narrow avenue of poplars, which commences near the palace gateway. A separate afternoon might be devoted to the above places; they may all be visited on horseback or in a dandy, and in the order in which they are named above. The hop *grounds*, in which the Maharajah has evinced so deep an interest, are also out in this direction.

The Chief Court or *Sadr-i-Dowlat* is on the right just below the *Shaikh Bàgh Ghàt;* the name of the present Judge is *Baboo Nilamber*, a native of Bengal.

The Ameeri Kadal is the first bridge down the river; and immediately below it, on the left, is a bazar for vegetables and grass.

The Sher Garhi contains the *city fort* and *royal palace*; it is built of stone, is rectangular in shape, about 400 yards long by 200 yards wide, and lies north-west and south-east; its walls are about 22 feet high, and strengthened at short intervals by stout bastions. The interior consists of an irregular assemblage of state apartments, dwelling-houses, Government offices, and barracks. The garrison is small, and consists partly of artillery with their guns. The southern and western sides are protected by a ditch about 30 feet wide; the northern is bounded by the *Kut-i-kul* Canal, and the river flows along its eastern side, where its walls support numerous wooden buildings which are chiefly occupied by the ministers and other high officials. The new and circular double-storied building upon one of the bastions overlooking the river is a part of the residence of the Prime Minister, *Dewan Kirpa Ram,* an able and acute statesman, a profound scholar, the author of several learned Persian Works, including an exhaustive treatise on Kashmir, and the son of *Dewan Jowalla Sàhài,* who has been for so many years the trusted and chief adviser of the present and late Mahárájahs. Immediately below it is the *toshakhana*—a long and lofty brick building with a grass-clad pent roof, containing shawls, *pushmeena,* treasure, and other valuable Government property. The *Rang Mehal*—a painted wooden room—stands next; it is a part of the Royal residence, and is used by the Maharajah as an audience hall. Just below it is the *Golghar,* or round house, a very capacious building, the finest modern structure in the city, and in which the Máharájah gives his evening entertainments to visitors, which are no less brilliant than sumptuous. Adjoining it is the *Royal temple* called the *Maharaj-ke-Mandir*, the roof of which is said to be covered with thin plates of pure gold.

The SUNT-I-KUL, or apple tree canal, is just opposite; it is about 30 yards wide, and is navigable for small boats all through the season; it is crossed by the *Gào Kadal*, and it leads to the *Chenàr Bàgh* and to the *Dal* or City Lake, from whence the water is derived.

The BASANT BAGH is next below this canal, and it has a very handsome *ghât* composed of limestone slabs, which were brought by the Sikh Governor *Meean Singh* from the mosque of *Hasanabad*, a suburb of the city: the garden is occupied by Hindoo *fakirs*, and there is a raised terrace inside it, where the Maharajah sometimes sits in the warm summer evenings to hold his *durbar*.

The KUT-I-KUL is the canal on the left, immediately below the *Sher Garhi*, which after passing through the western portion of the city re-enters the river below the *Naya Kadal* or sixth bridge; it is about the same width as the *Sunt-i-kul* but not so deep: the *Tainki Kadal* is seen crossing it a few yards from the river.

The Colonel BEEJA SINGH-KI-MANDIR is the new temple immediately below and on the right.

The GANPATYAR-KE-MANDIR is also a new temple situated a little lower down on the right, and was built by *Wazeer Púnu*, the Governor of Kashmir.

The HABBA KADAL is the next or second bridge, and it was the most curious of them all, having a row of wooden shops all along both sides, like the old London Bridge; they were burnt down in 1870.

The MEAN SAHIB-KI-MANDIR, perhaps the largest modern temple in Kashmir, is on the left, a little below the above bridge; the number of Hindu temples has been much increased during the present reign.

A BUDDHIST INSCRIPTION may be found upon the end of a stone in the foundation of a house adjoining the upper side of the *Mallikyar*, a *ghât* on the left and a little below the above temple; the stone is 17 inches broad and 13½ inches high, and is situated about two feet above the bed of the river, so that it is only visible when the water is low.

The next or third bridge is the *Fati Kadal*; just above it on the left is the warehouse of *Sonoo Shah*, Shawl merchant and banker, immediately opposite which is the *Diwan-ki-Mandir*; just below it, on the left, is the warehouse of *Mookteah Shàh*, a Government Shawl agent; on the right, and nearly opposite, is that of *Syfoola Bàba*; and on the left, about 200 yards lower down, is that of *Sammad Shah*, both shawl merchants and bankers, and who would readily conduct the visitor to some of the shawl-weaving rooms in the vicinity of their premises.

The SHAH HAMADAN MASJID is situated on the right, and just below the *Fati Kadal*; it is one of the most elaborate as well as one of the most celebrated mosques in Kashmir. Inside it there is a Persian inscription which runs thus: "All temporal and spiritual good can be obtained by being a follower of *Shàh Hamadàn*; he has control over all the affairs of this world; whoever doubts this shall be blinded." Another reads thus: "Oh my soul! If thou wouldst obtain thine object in this world and the next, go to the gate of *Hamadán*; by going to that gate thou shalt reach heaven; this gate is a symbol of the heavenly throne." The top of it commands a magnificent view of the city. Like all the mosques of Kashmir, it is built of cedar with a golden ball on the top instead of the Mohamedan crescent; ornamental bell flowers, carved in wood, are hung around the projecting roof.

The BAGHI-DILAWUR KHAN is an old Pathan garden, about five minutes' walk from the *ghât* adjoining the *Sháh Hamadán*, and is situated on the edge of the *Dal* or City Lake, or rather a branch of it, from which it may also be visited by water. It is about 128 yards long and 70 yards wide, and is interesting to the visitor as having been the residence of the travellers HUGEL, VIGNE, and HENDERSON, during their stay in Srinagar in 1835. Jacquemont also stayed here. It has lately been put in order, and several new buildings have been erected for the use of *special* visitors only.

The No MASJID, or PATARMASJID, is on the left bank of the river and nearly opposite the *Sháh Hamadán;* it was once a very fine building of polished limestone, and was built by *Núr Jehán Begum*—the beautiful *Núrmahal,* or Light of the Harem, of Lalla Rookh; its interior, which was formerly paved with stone, is about 60 yards long and 18 yards wide, and is divided into three passages by two rows of massive stone arches, which extend from one end to the other; it is now used only as a granary.

Adjoining the fine old *ghát* leading to this mosque is a *burial ground,* where three or four massive fluted limestone columns are lying about; and near them is an old zearut, called the *Háji Ahmedi Khári.*

The ZAINA KADAL is the next or fourth bridge, and it supports a row of wooden shops on both sides of the right two-thirds of its length. The *Shaikh Mussa-ke-masjid* is just below it on the left.

The BADSHAH is one of the oldest and most interesting ruins in the city; it is built of brick and is situated on the right, just below the above bridge; it is the tomb of *Zainul Abodin*, who, as previously stated, lived in the early part of the 15th century, and was the eighth and most renowned of the *Bádshahs* or Mahomedan Kings of Kashmir. Shawls are said to have been first made in his reign by weavers brought from *Turkestan*, and the *Lanka* in the *Woolar Lake* is attributed to him; the adjoining bridge and many other places in the country also bear his name. The tomb is surrounded by a burial-ground, which is enclosed by a massive stone wall having a fine arched entrance on the south-eastern side; on the north-western side, and near the middle of the wall, is a raised tomb about 3 feet high, upon which is a flat stone, 2 feet wide and 4¾ feet long, bearing an inscription written by order of *Moorcroft* the traveller, and recording the conquest of Kashmir by *Mirza Hyder Goorkhán*, a relative of *Aboo Said Khan, Bádshah of Yarkund*, and foster brother of the Emperor *Humayun*, with 400 cavalry from *Yarkund viâ Ladak*, about A.D. 1512, and again with 450 cavalry from *Lahore*, about A.D. 1520, as previously mentioned.

The JUMMA MUSJEED, or GREAT MOSQUE, is about eight minutes' walk from the *Bádshah Ghât*, and it may also be reached from the *Már Canal*. According to the inscription outside the entrance, it was built by the Emperor *Shah Jehan*. It is a very large four-sided building, with an open square in the centre, and a wooden steeple in the middle of each side; the roof of the surrounding cloister is supported by wooden pillars, each formed of a single *deodar* tree about 30 feet high, and resting upon a plain stone base; there are three rows upon the north, south, and west sides, but only two on the eastern side. On the west side a fine Gothic arch opens from the square to the altar, over which the roof is much higher than in any other part; the north and south sides are 120 yards long and about 20 yards wide; the east and west sides are 118 yards long; the width of the former is 16 yards, and the latter 22 yards: the floor is paved throughout with bricks placed edgeways.

Nearly opposite to the entrance to this Mosque there is a *raised stone platform* covered with graves, and close to it a small *ruined enclosure,* the remains of a temple; a little further on is a very large and deep *tank* having a long and broad flight of steps leading down to the water. Outside the western wall of the Mosque there are several *Chak tombs,* amongst which is a small miniature temple with four sides, each of which is about 12 inches wide and 18 inches high; it is supported upon a fluted stone column $2\frac{1}{4}$ feet high and 3 feet 8 inches in circumference. About four minutes' walk to the north-north-west of the Mosque, and just beyond the ruin called the *Pir Haji Mahomed,* there is a very large *hak burial-ground* containing many curious and ancient monuments. The *Chaks,* as previously mentioned, were a noble family, and some of them became Kings of Kashmir.

The MINT, or ZERAB KHANA, is only two or three minutes' walk from the *Badshah Ghat,* and is a small mean-looking building surrounded by ordinary dwelling-houses. The mode of coining is on a par with the simplicity of the buildings; the quantities necessary for each coin are cut from the bars of metal, and, when weighed, are made over to another workman to be beaten into shape; for this purpose he puts each piece into a small charcoal fire contained in a *kangri,* and when sufficiently heated, he takes it out with a small pair of tongs, and holding it upon an anvil with the left hand, hammers it into a nummular form with the right; it is then stamped with a die, which, while held upon the piece by one man's hand, receives from another a single but heavy blow from a large hammer. Arrangements have lately been made for a new mintage and coinage, at Jamoo, and new silver coins are already in circulation.

The MAHARAJ GANGE, a fine large Bazar, is immediately below the *Badshah,* and has been recently built for the convenience of visitors desirous of purchasing the various Kashmirian manufactures. Adjoining it is the CITY SCHOOL, and near it the Printing Office of the *Tofa-i-Kashmir,* a weekly newspaper of great interest.

The RAINTAN SHAH-KE-MASJID is an old stone building on the right, immediately below the next bridge or ALLI KADAL, and it bears a peculiar *inscription* in the *Nagri* character, supposed to be *Bhuddist*; it may be found upon the end of a stone in the middle of the outer side of the western wall, about 6 feet above the ground. The *Wysee Sahib-ke-Zearat* is just below this building.

The BULBUL LANKAR is a very old wooden mosque on the right, about 200 yards below the *Alli Kadal*; it is said to have been the first erected in Kashmir, and to contain the ashes of the *fakir* named *Búlbul Shah,* by whom Mahomedanism is said to have been introduced into the country in the 12th century: trees are growing through the roof of the building, which until lately was in a ruinous and neglected state.

THE NAYA KADAL is the next or sixth bridge, and about 300 yards below it, on the right, is an old brick building called the *Dudmood Khan-ke-Masjid.* Just below this again, on the same side, is the mansion of the late *Pundit Raj Kak,* the minister of shawls, to whom was attributed the serious outbreak of the weavers in Srinagar on the 20th April 1865; shortly after this event he died suddenly, and from careful enquiries made by the author, most probably from a paralytic stroke.

The THAGGI BABA-KE-ZEARAT or *Mallick Sahib* is nearly opposite this house, and immediately above the junction of the *Kut-i-kul* Canal with the river; it contains some marble tombs, and some exquisite specimens of lattice-work in plaister of Paris, and should be visited.

The EEDGAH, the place at which the great assemblies of the Mohamedans are held during their religious festivals, is about ten minutes' walk from the ghât called *Lachmanjew-ke-Yaribal*, which is on the right, and about 100 yards above the last bridge or *Suffa Kadal:* it is a beautiful park-like plain, smooth, level, and carpetted with fine grass, about a mile in length and a quarter of a mile in width, surrounded by large trees, and bounded on the east by the *Mar Canal*; it is the prettiest spot about the city, and has been well compared to an English village green. At its northern end there is a fine old wooden mosque called the *Alli Masjid,* which is half concealed by some of the largest *chenárs* in Kashmir, one of them being in 1865, 32 feet in circumference; the interior is about 64 yards long and 22 wide; the roof is flat, and supported by four rows of polygonal wooden pillars, each resting upon a plain triangular stone pedestal about 18 inches high; upon the floor, near the western wall, there was a stone slab, 3 feet long and 15 inches high, bearing an Arabic inscription stating that this *Alli Masjid* wns built in the time of *Sultan Hassxin Bádshah* by *Kaji Hasti, Sondr*, about A.D. 1471. Nearly opposite the above ghat (or *Yaribal*, as a landing place is called in Kashmir) is the warehouse for Central Asian Merchandize, lately erected by order of the Máharájah.

The SUFFA KADAL is the last bridge, and immediately below it, on the left, is the *Zearat of Shah Naimatullah*, which contains a stone slab with an inscription upon it, stating that the adjoining bridge was built by *Saif Khan* in A.D. 1664: hence its name. A little lower down is the mouth of the *Dudhgunga* or the *Chassa Kul*, and below it again is the *Noor Bagh*—the place of execution—where the old gallows formerly stood; capital punishment however has not been inflicted in Kashmir for many years.

If the water is high enough, the visitor may return by the *Kut-i-Kul* Canal, which enters the left bank of the river immediately below the zearut of *Thaggi Baba*; it intersects the southern portion of the city and is crossed by several bridges, the principal of which is the *Tainki Kadal* near the *Sher Garhi*, where it rejoins the river.

The Dal or City Lake.

The Dal or City Lake may next be visited and several days might be most agreeably spent in examining the various places of interest in and around it: it is one of the most renowned portions of Kashmir, and of which Moore in his *Lalla Rookh* thus exclaims :—

Oh! best of delights, as it every where is,
To be near the loved *one*, what a rapture is his,
Who in moonlight and music thus sweetly may glide
O'er the lake of Cashmere with that *one* by his side!
If woman can make the worst wilderness dear?
Think, think what a heaven she must make of Cashmere.

It is situated on the north-eastern side of the city, and may be reached by water from the *Sunt-í-Kul* or Apple-tree Canal, which flows into the river opposite the *Sher Garhi*; it is about 5 miles long, 2½ miles broad, and its average depth is about 10 feet; its northern and eastern sides are bounded by green and lofty mountains, which slope down to within a mile or so of its margin and its different portions have received separate names. The water, which is very clear, is chiefly derived from springs; but a considerable stream from the hills enters its northern side. Its surface is in many parts covered with floating gardens, also the lotus and *singhara* plants, and tall rushes; it contains fish, and in the autumn months it abounds with wild fowl of all kinds.

Time Table for Journeys to places about the Lake in a Shikàrah with a crew of six men.

Time occupied.	From To	To From	Time occupied.
30 minutes	Moonshi Bágh.	Sher Garhi	20 minutes.
40 ditto	ditto	Chenár Bágh	40 ditto
50 ditto	ditto	Drógjun	50 ditto
20 ditto	Drógjun	Naiwidyár	26 ditto
50 ditto	ditto	Hazratbal	1 hour
1 hour	ditto	Naseeb Bágh	1¼ ditto
1 ditto	ditto	Isle of Chenàrs	1¼ ditto
1¼ ditto	ditto	Shálimár Bágh	1½ ditto
1 ditto	ditto	Nishat Bágh	1¼ ditto
40 minutes	ditto	Chasma Sháhi	45 minutes.

The Sunt-i-Kul is a very pretty canal connecting the *Dal* with the *Jhelam*; at its lower end, opposite the *Sher Garhi*, it is about 30 yards wide, and varies in depth from 3 to 15 feet, according to the height of the river. Its upper end winds round by the *Moonshi Bagh*, where it is narrower and not so deep, and terminates about 20 feet from the river. The *Gáo Kádal* crosses it near the *Sher Garhi* end. It is embanked on both sides and lined with magnificent trees, chiefly chenars and poplars; its surface is covered with numbers of tame ducks and geese, the property of the Maharajah. The *powder manufactory* is a little above the *Gáo Kadal,* and the State barges are usually moored close to it.

The Chenar Bagh is on the left bank of this canal, and about twenty minutes' journey by boat from the *Sher Garhi*; this fine grove of *chenars* is a favorite place for encampment, but it is liable to be inundated when the river rises very high.

Drogjun is a small village adjoining the water-gate of the Dal, and is about thirty-six minutes' journey form the *Sher Garhi.* When the river is low, the gates called the *Dal-ke-Darwaza* remain open, but when it rises to a certain height, they close of themselves, thus preventing inundation of the land around the lake. There is a bridge over the flood-gates, and a causeway leading from it, both of which were constructed by the Pathans. The *Dal-ke-Darwaza* is a favorite place for bathing and fishing; the water varies in depth from 15 to 40 feet, and abounds with small fish resembling the trout.

On entering the lake several channels will be seen passing between the tall rushes; but to visit the places in the order in which they are here described; the channel leading directly northwards must be selected, it is well known to the boatmen.

The Nalli Mar is a canal running off to the left, soon after passing *Drógjun*; it flows through the northern portion of the city, and empties itself into the *Anchar Lake*, which is connected with the *Sind* river; it resembles the old canals in Venice; its average width is about 20 feet, and boats can pass along it during the greater part of the season; it is crossed by several old-fashioned stone bridges, and is fringed in many places with trees, and festooned with vines, the *Bagh-i-Dilawar Khan*, the *Mint* and the *Jamma Másjid* may be visited from it. On its left bank is the *Dagh Shawl*, where all the Shawls must be brought to be stamped, failing which a severe penalty involving imprisonment is incurred.

Shawl-washing is carried on near the small village of *Budmarg*, on the left bank of the lake, and about a quarter of an hour's journey from *Drogjun*; the shawls are beaten upon large blocks of limestone, of which there are about twenty, the remains of an old building which formerly stood near the spot.

Kraleeyar is the name of the large village about half a mile further on; there are several ruins and some very fine old ghats near it, and good fishnig may be had above the wooden bridge which here crosses the canal.

The Naiwidyar is a stone bridge about half an hour's journey from *Drógjun*, and consists of three elegant arches; there is a small marble slab on each side of the middle arch bearing a Persian inscription.

The SUTOO is an artificial causeway extending completely across the lake; it commences on the right of the *Naiwidyár Bridge,* and terminates at the southern side of the village of *Isheeburi,* close to the northern side of the *Nishat Bagh;* it is about 4 miles long, its average width is 12 feet, and there are nine bridges along its course, two of which are of stone and seven of wood; it has given way in several places, at two of which it is difficult to cross, so that it is unfit for ponies and ladies, and only fit for walking; the journey from one end to the other occupies about an hour and a quarter.

HASSANABAD is a fine old ruined mosque on the left, about 200 yards above the *Naiwidyár,* and near the bank of the canal, a branch of which runs along its eastern side, from whence it may be reached by a flight of stone steps. It was built by the *Shiahs* in the time of *Akbar*, and was composed of bricks and mortar, enfaced within and without by large and elaborately carved masses of limestone, after the style of the *Pattar Masjid.* The Sikh Governor, *Mean Singh,* demolished it, and, as previously mentioned, the blocks of limestone were carried away to form the noble ghat at the *Bassant Bagh,* opposite the *Sher Garhi.* An interesting cemetery is attached to it, and near it, on the south, is a pretty little wooden mosque recently built by the *Sunis,* the rival sect of Mohammedans. This village was the scene of that sad religious strife—bloodshed, fire, and wholesale plunder—which occurred last year (1874) between the *Sunis* and *Shiahs*.

Some of the celebrated FLOATING GARDENS will be seen about a mile beyond the *Naiwidyár*, covering a very large extent of this portion of the lake; they are chiefly devoted to the cultivation of melons and cucumbers, and are formed in the following manner :—

"The roots of aquatic plants growing in shallow places are divided about 2 feet under the water, so that they completely lose all connection with the bottom of the lake, but retain their former situation in respect to each other. When thus detached from the soil they are pressed into somewhat closer contact, and formed into beds of about 2 yards in breadth, and of an indefinite length. The heads of the sedges, reeds, and other plants of the floats are now cut off and laid upon its surface, and covered with a thin coat of mud, which at first intercepted in its descent, gradually sinks into the mass of matted roots. The bed floats, but is kept in its place by a stake of willow driven through it at each end, which admits of its rising or falling in accommodation to the rise or fall of the water."—*Vide* Moorcroft, Vol. II., page 137.

HAZRATBAL is a large village on the western side of the lake, and a little more than half an hour's journey from the *Naiwidyar ;* it has a fine flight of stone steps along its whole front, and is famed throughout Kashmir for its very sacred *Zearat,* which contains a reputed relic of Mohamet, in the form of a hair of the prophet's beard, enclosed in a small silver box covered by a glass lid. Four festivals are held here annually, during which the relic is exhibited to the credulous thousands who assemble from all parts of the valley; the chief one occurs in August, when the lake swarms with boats of all kinds, which are filled with gaily dressed devotees of both sexes, of all ages, and of all ranks: the scene is very picturesque and well worth witnessing. The Feast of Roses was in former times one of the most important of these festivals, and it was during one of these that the famous love-quarrel occurred between the *Emperor Jehangir* and his beautiful wife, the celebrated *Núrmahal,* concerning which the poet *Moore* thus writes:—

Alas how light a cause may move,
Dissension between hearts that love!
Hearts that the world in vain has tried,
And sorrow but more closely tied;
That stood the storm when waves were rough,
Yet in a sunny hour fall off,

Like ships that have gone down at sea,
When heaven was all tranquillity!
A something light as air—a look,
A word unkind, or wrongly taken—
Oh! love that tempests never shook,
A breath, a touch like this has shaken!
And ruder words will soon rush in,
To spread the breach that words begin,
And eyes forget the gentle ray,
They wore in courtship's smiling day;
And voices lose the tone that shed,
A tenderness round all they said;
Till fast declining, one by one,
The sweetnesses of love are gone,
And hearts, so lately mingled, seem
Like broken clouds or like the stream,
That smiling left the mountain's brow,
As though its waters ne'er could sever,
Yet ere it reach the plain below,
Breaks into floods that part for ever!

* * * * * *

The NASSEEB BAGH, or *Garden of Bliss*, is a favorite place for picnics: it is a magnificent grove of *chenars* situated a few hundred yards beyond *Hazratbal*, and about 1¼ hours' journey by boat from *Drógjun;* it is said to have been planted in the time of *Akbar*, and was formerly about half a mile long, a quarter of a mile wide, and was probably surrounded by a wall of masonry. In front of it, on the edge of the lake, are the remains of an extensive embankment, a flight of stone steps, and other works of stone.

The Char Chenar or Isle of Chenars—called also the *Rupa Lank* or *Silver Island*—is situated opposite the *Nasseeb Bagh*, and in the middle of the northern portion of the lake; it was the fancy of *Nur Begum*, the wife of *Jehangir*, and is mentioned in the works of *Bernier* and *Moore*. It is a mass of masonry, 46 yards square, and about 3 feet above the water: there was originally a masonry platform for a *siesta*, and a plane tree at each corner, to give shade at any time of the day, hence its name the Four Chenars. *Vigne* visited it in November 1835, and says there was then a small square temple upon it with marble pillars, surrounded by a little garden filled with flowers; the temple and garden are no longer there; the black marble tablet, which he states was put up, has also disappeared: he tells us it bore the following inscription:—

Three Travellers,
Baron Carl Von Hugel, from Jamu,
John Henderson, from Ladak,
Godfrey Thomas Vigne, from Iskardo,
Who met in Srinagar on the 18th November 1835,
Have caused the names of those European travellers who had previously visited the Vale of Kashmir to be hereunder engraved:
Bernier, 1663.
Forster, 1786.

MOORCROFT, TREBECK, and GUTHRIE, 1823.
JACQUEMONT, 1831.
WOLFF, 1832.
Of these, three only lived to return to their native country.

The JAIL is situated a few hundred yards beyond the *Nuseeb Bagh*, and adjoining the village of *Habbag;* it was an old pleasure garden called *Saif Khan Bagh;* the huts or barracks are built upon the lower terrace, which is open all round, but protected by a guard of sepoys. The prisoners are well clothed and fed; their fetters, which vary in weight according to their offences, are not very heavy, and their labor, which is chiefly that of grinding corn, is by no means severe.

TELBAL is the name of that small village beyond the jail, and at the northern side of the lake.

The SHALMIAR BAGH is a fine old pleasure garden made by the Emperor *Jehangir*, and is situated at the north-eastern corner of the lake, with which it is connected by an artificial canal 12 yards wide and about a mile long. On each side of this canal are broad and green paths, which are overshadowed by trees, chiefly willows and chenars, and at its junction with the lake there are blocks of masonry on both sides, which indicate the site of the old gateway; there are also the remains of a stone embankment which formerly lined the canal throughout. The *Shalimar* is 590 yards long, and its width at the lower end 207 yards, while that of the upper end is 267 yards; it is surrouuded by a brick and stone wall about 10 feet high, and is arranged in four terraces lying one above another and of nearly equal dimensions. There is a line of tanks or reservoirs along the middle of the whole length of the garden, and they are connected by a canal 18 inches deep and from 9 to 14 yards wide. The tanks and the canal are lined with polished limestone resembling black marble, and filled with large and beautiful fountains. The water is derived from a stream which rises in the mountains behind the garden; it enters at its upper end, and flows down from each successive terrace in cascades, which are received into the reservoirs below, and which contain nnmerous fountains; after leaving the garden, it falls into the outer canal, by which it is conducted to the lake.

The uppermost or fourth terrace was the private portion of the garden, where the princesses and other ladies of the imperial *Zenana* disported themselves in its palmy days. It is much higher than the others, and is enclosed all round by a wall, in the lower portion of which are two gateways, reached by a lofty flight of steps on each side of the central canal. In its centre there is a magnificent black marble pavilion, which is raised upon a platform a little more than 3 feet high and 65 feet square; its roof is flat, about 20 feet high, and supported on each side by a row of six elaborately carved black marble pillars, which are of polygonal shape and fluted; on two sides there is an open corridor, 65 feet long and 18 feet wide, and in the centre an open passage about 26 feet long and 21 feet wide, on the right and left of which is a closed apartment about 21 feet long and 13 feet wide. This pavilion is surrounded by a fine reservoir 52 yards square and about 3½ feet deep; it is lined with stone, and contains 144 large fountains. Upon each side of this principal terrace, and built against the wall, there is also a lodge; these formed the private apartments of the imperial family. On each of the three lower terraces there is also a small pavilion which overlooks the fountains in the tank below; each consists of two apartments, one on each side of the canal, over which there is a covered archway uniting the two, and that on the lowest terrace is supported by sixteen black pillars, fluted, and of polygonal shape.

The *Shalimar* is a favorite place for dinners, picnics, balls, and other entertainments; and when, at night, the fountains are playing, and the canal, its waterfalls, the numerous pavilions, and the whole garden, are illuminated with colored lamps, the effect is beautiful and beyond description. It was the *Trianon* of the old Mogul Emperors. Here the Emperor *Jehangir* spent many days and nights of many summers with the fair *Núrmahal,* who lies burried in the *Taj* at Agra, and here was the scene of their reconciliation as given in the following lines of Moore's "*Light of the Haram.*"

That evening (trusting that his soul
Might be from haunting love released)
By mirth, by music, and the bowl)
Th' imperial Selim held a feast
In his magnificent Shálimár ;—

Thither *Núrmahal* repairs after having invoked the aid of the witch *Namouna;* she is masked and disguised as an *Arabian minstrel,* and being admitted to the presence outvies all the other singers, quite eclipsing a lovely *Georgian maid,* who sings the following song :—

" Come hither, come hither—by night and by day
We linger in pleasures that never are gone ;
Like the waves of the summer, as one dies away,
Another as sweet and as shining comes on.
And the love that is o'er, in expiring gives birth,
To a new one as warm, as unequalled in bliss ;
And oh ! if there be an Elysium on earth,
It is this, it is this."

" Here maidens are sighing, and fragrant their sigh
As the flower of the Amra just oped by the bee,
And precious their tears as that rain from the sky,
Which turns into pearls as it falls in the sea ;

Oh! think what the kiss and smile must be worth,
When the sigh and the tear are so perfect in bliss,
And own, if there be an Elysium on earth
It is this, it is this."

These verses *Nurmahal* parodies with the following beautiful song:—

"There's a bliss beyond all that the minstrel has told,
When two that are linked in one heavenly tie,
With hearts never changing, and brow never cold,
Love on through all ills and love on till they die!
One hour of a passion so sacred is worth
Whole ages of heartless and wandering bliss;
And oh! if there be an Elysium on earth
It is this, it is this.

At once a hundred voices said:
"It is the masked Arabian maid!"
While Selim who had felt the same
Deepest of any, and had lain
Some minutes rapt as in a trance
After the fairy sounds were o'er.
Too inly touched for utterance,
Now motioned with his hand for more.

Nurmahal then sang another song, the effects of which upon her spouse were still more powerful, and which the poet *Moore* thus describes.

There was a pathos in this lay,
That even, without enchantment's art,
Would instantly have found its way,
Deep into Selim's burning heart;

But breathing, as it did, a tone
To earthly lutes and lips unknown,
With every chord fresh from the touch
Of music's spirit,—'twas too much!
Starting, he dashed away the cup,—
Which all the time of this sweet air,
His hand had held, untasted up,
 As if 'twere fixed by magic there,—
And naming her, so long unnamed,
So long unseen, wildly exclaimed,
"O Nurmahal! O Nurmahal!
Hadst thou but sung this witching strain,
I could forget, forgive thee all,
And never leave those eyes again!"

The mask is off the charm is wrought—
And Selim to his heart has caught,
In blushes, more than ever bright,
His Nurmahal, his Harem's Light!
And well do vanished frowns enhance
The charm of every brighten'd glance;
And dearer seems each dawning smile
For having lost its light awhile;
And happier now for all her sighs,
 As on his arm, her head reposes,
She whispers him, with laughing eyes,
"Remember love, the Feast of Roses!

ISHEEBURI is the name of the village just below the *Shalimar*, on the eastern side of the lake. The cause-way extending across the lake, and called the *Sutoo*, terminates at the southern side of this village, which contains a very sacred spring called *Ganga*, at which a large assembly takes place annually of Pandits, and Hindus generally.

The NISHAT BAGH—another favorite place for picnics and other parties—is a fine old pleasure garden like the *Shalimar*, and was also made by the Emperor *Jehangir;* it is situated near the middle of the eastern margin of the lake, and is reached by passing under one of the bridges on the *Sutoo*. The fine poplars growing all round it, and the large pavilion on the edge of its lower terrace, render it conspicuous at a great distance, but, as in the case of the *Shalimar* and the *Chashma Shahi*, visitors are not allowed to take up their abode in it. It is about 595 yards long, 360 yards wide, and is surrounded by a stone and brick wall, which on the front side is 13 feet high. It is arranged in ten terraces, the upper three of which are much higher than the others, being from 16 to 18 feet, one above the other. There is a line of tanks along the centre of the whole garden, and they are connected by a canal about 13 feet wide and 8 inches deep; the tanks and the canal are lined with polished limestone, and contain numerous fountains, and on each side of the canal there is a grassy path about 12 feet wide. The water is derived from the same stream which supplies the *Shalimar;* it enters the upper end of the garden, and flows down the successive terraces in cascades formed by inclined walls of masonry, which are covered with limestone slabs, and beautifully scalloped to vary the appearance of the water; some of these are very fine, being from 12 to 18 feet high.

There are two principal pavilions, one at the lower, and the other at the upper, end of the garden. The *lower pavilion* is double-storied, and built upon a foundation of stone; in the middle of its lower floor there is a reservoir about 14 feet square, 3 feet deep, and filled with fountains, which are visible through an opening in the upper story. It has lately been completely renovated, indeed the Maharajah seems to be doing much towards restoring these *Old Mogul Pleasure Gardens* throughout the valley, which is not the least of the many signs of progress on the part of the present Government.

The *upper pavilion* is situated upon the edge of the highest terrace, and consists of a double-storied building on each side of the canal, over which is a closed passage uniting the two. The lower story of each building contains one room 26 feet long and 10½ feet wide; the upper story also contains one room, which is 26 feet long and 13 feet wide. The passage between them is supported on each side of the canal by a fine row of wooden pillars painted red and green; it is 43 feet long, 36 feet wide, and about 40 feet high. On the terrace below this pavilion there is also a very fine reservoir, 102 feet wide, 123 long, 3 feet deep, and containing twenty-five large fountains.

BREN is the name of the pretty village which is situated on the slope of the mountain near the southern side of the *Nishat Bagh.*

The SONA LANK or GOLDEN ISLAND is situated in the middle of the southern portion of the lake, and about twenty minutes' row from the *Nishat.* It is an artificial mass of masonry, originally built by one of the Mogul Emperors as a companion to the Rupa Lank. It is 40 yards long and 36 yards wide, and its sides are green and slope gently down to the edge of the water. The centre is occupied by the foundations and part of the walls of an old square building, which, until lately, was used as the jail—a very secure place for this purpose, escape by swimming being impossible, owing to the reeds and other plants growing in the bed of the lake. The ruins are half concealed by mulberry trees and blackberry bushes, and the ground is completely undermined by a colony of rats.

The CHASMA SHAHI is a famous spring in a small pleasure garden situated on the side of the hills and nearly a mile from the south-eastern margin of the lake. The garden is about 113 yards long and 42 yards wide, and is surrounded by a wall about 7 feet high. It is arranged upon the same plan as the *Shalimar* and *Nishat;* there are three terraces, a central canal, tanks, waterfalls, and fountains, which are all supplied from the spring which is situated at the southern end of the garden, and is justly esteemed for its coolness and great purity. A wooden pavilion or *baradaree* occupies the lower end of the middle terrace; it is double-storied, and the lower is divided lengthwise into two rooms, the posterior of which contains a fine reservoir and a fountain; the upper story consists of a central room about 16 by 14 feet, opening on each side by trellised arches, into a varandah enclosed by beautiful latice-work made of wood. The canal passes under the basement story, and after leaving the reservoir falls into the lower terrace in a fine cascade about 16 feet high.

The PERI MAHAL or KUTLUN is an old ruin standing upon the side of a spur of the lofty mountains on the southern side of the lake; it is situated above the village of *Theed*, about a mile from the margin of the lake, and consists of seven long ranges of buildings composed of stone and arranged in terraces; it is attributed to *Akhun Mulla Shah*, the tutor or spiritual guide of the Emperor *Jehan Gir*, who is said to have designed it as a college. The ascent from *Theed* is easy, even for ponies, and occupies about twenty minutes; the ruin commands a splended view of the lake.

The SHAKH SAFAI BAGH is the garden beyond the village of *Theed;* it contains two brick-built bungalows, one at each end, which are both private, and belong to a pundit.

A little further on is the *gulee* between the *Panduchak* and the *Takht-i-Suliman* through which leads the pony-road which passes round the lake. After proceeding a short distance along the foot of the *Takht* the *Drógjun* again comes in sight, and on the left of it is a mound which formerly supported a watch-tower called *Rustam Garhi*, the remains of which may still be seen. Upon turning to the left, after returning through the *Drógjun*, a bridge will be reached in the course of a few minutes, which crosses this part of the *Sunt-i-Kul;* it is close to the upper end of the *poplar avenue*, through which the visitor may enjoy a short and pleasant walk back to the bungalows.

The BRIDLE ROAD AROUND THE LAKE passes through the gap in the hills behind the upper or married range of bungalows, and the following table gives the average time occupied, at an ordinary walking pace, in reaching some of the different places along its edge :—

From	To	Time.
Munshi Bàgh.	Gap below the Tukht	18 minutes.
Ditto	Shaikh Safái Bágh	32 ditto.
Ditto	Theed	40 ditto.
Ditto	Chashma Sháhi	55 ditto.
Ditto	Bren	1 hour.
Ditto	Nishát Bágh	1½ ditto.
Ditto	Isheeburi	1¾ ditto.
Ditto	Shálimár	2 ditto.

CHAPTER IV.

EASTERN PORTION OF KASHMIR.

The original of the Shawl pattern—Rám Moonshi Bágh—Vathnar Nálli—Pándritan—Pándú Chakk—Pámpoor—Mineral Springs—Iron Works—Ladoo ruins—Kárkerpore—Páyech Temple—Kohil ruin—Awantipore Tráahal—Veshau River—Samma Thang—Bijbehára—Liddar River Kanbal—Korwinee—Islamabad—Mártand—Bawan—Caves of Bhoomjoo—Achibal to Nowboog—Nowboog to Kookar Nág—Kookar Nág to Vernág—Vernág to Rozloo—Rozloo to Ban Doosar—Ban Doosar to Nohán—Nohán to Shupiyan—Shupiyan to Chràr—Chrár to Srinagar—Liddár Valley and Cave of Ambarnath—Wardwan Valley.

The chief places of interest in the eastern portion of Kashmir are the principal springs and sources of the *Jhelam*, the magnificent *ruins of Martand, Awantipore* and others, and some beautiful minor valleys, as the *Nowboog, Liddar, Wardwan* and others. A part of this tour—that from *Srinagar* to *Kanbal*, near *Islamabad*—may be accomplished by water; the visitor may engage one or more *doongahs* for himself and servants, and the horses can march along the banks of the river, orders being given to the syces where to halt.

Time table for journeys by Doongah to places on the River east of Srinagar.

Average time occupied.	From To	To From	Average time occupied.
4½ hours.	Srinagar.	Pámpoor ...	7 hours.
12 „	Do.	Awantipore ...	15 „
16 „	Do.	Bijbehára ...	24 „
18 „	Do.	Kanbal ...	28 „

List of Stages in the Eastern Tour of the Valley.

From	To	Distance.	Remarks.
Srinagar ...	Kanbal ...	By boat.	In about two days.
Islamabad ...	Báwan ...	5 miles	Easy road.
Islamabád ...	Achibal ...	6 „	Ditto.
Atchibal ...	Nowboog ...	12 „	Cross a range of hills.
Nowbook ...	Kookar Nág ...	12 „	Tolerably easy road.
Kookar Nág...	Vernág ...	7½ „	Cross a range of hills.
Vernág ...	Rozloo ...	8 „	Easy road.
Rozloo ...	Ban Doosar ...	10¼ „	Rather rough road.
Ban Doosar...	Nohán ...	10½ „	Ditto ditto.
Nohán ...	Shupiyan ...	13 „	Easy road.
Shupiyan ...	Chrár ...	13½ „	Easy but undulating road.
Chrár ...	Srinagar ...	15 „	Ditto ditto.

Three or four BEAUTIFUL CURVES take place in the river soon after passing above the *Moonshi Bágh*, and the boats seem to make slow progress along the base of the mountains which stretch from the *Takht-i-Suliman*;

these curves, as seen from the top of that hill, are said to be the originals of the figures upon the Kashmir shawls, the pattern of which is so well known.

The RAM MOONSHI BAGH is a large orchard on the right bank of the river, and about half an hour's journey by boat above the *Moonshi Bágh;* it contains chiefly apples, pears, mulberries, and grapes, and is a pleasant and salubrious place for a few days' encampment.

The VATHNAR NALLI is a canal about 20 feet wide, which enters the left bank of the river about five minutes' rowing above the *Ram Moonshi Bágh;* about half a mile from its mouth are some floodgates adjoining a small village, where there is excellent fishing.

PANDRITAN—a corruption of *Puran Adi Sthan*—was once the capital of Kashmir, and it extended along the foot of the mountains for about 3 miles; it contained a famous shrine founded by *Asoka*, grandson of *Chundra Gupta,* who reigned from B.C. 263 to 226, and it enshrined a tooth of *Buddha,* which had to be given up about A.D. 630 to the powerful King of *Kanouj*. The King *Abhimanyu,* Nero-like, set fire to it, and the site is strewn with ruined masses, amongst which is the lower portion of the legs and feet of a sitting colossal statue formerly about 20 feet high. One of the temples being situated in a tank—like all the old temples, to put them under the protection of the *Nágas*—escaped;

it is behind a grove of willows about 50 yards from the right bank of the river, and adjoining a village which is only about half an hour's walk above the *Moonshi Bágh*, but by water about 2½ hours' journey. The temple, which is one of the most interesting archæological specimens in Kashmir, is built of stone, and is pyramidal in shape; each side is 15 feet broad, and has a trefoil arched opening; the interior is hollow, and the roof is most elaborately sculptured; the tank surrounding it, now filled with tall rushes, is about 40 yards square.

PANDU CHACKK is the place where the spur of the hill reaches the right bank of the river, about an hour and a half's journey by boat above *Pándritan;* the remains of a stone bridge are seen here, which, according to an inscription upon a loose slab, lying on the right bank, was built in the time of the Emperor *Jehan Gir*.

PAMPOOR—founded by *Padma* between A.D. 832 and 844—is a large and dilapidated town, situated on the right bank of the river, about 8 miles by land above the *Moonshi Bágh*, and about six or seven hours' journey by boat. A wooden bridge crosses the river opposite the town, which contains a fine old mosque and a *zearat;* there is a large orchard on the right bank just below the town, and a fine grove of *chénars* between the bridge and the town, both of which are suitable for encamping.

A *Royal Lodge* for the use of the Maharajah, has lately been built upon the river-side.

Saffron—called *Zaffrán* or *Késar*, the stamina of the flowers of the *Crocus sativus*—is extensively cultivated upon the *Kareewahs* or *Wudirs* around *Pámpoor;* it is chiefly used as a dye, but is also an article of food, and yields a large revenue. The plants are arranged in small parterres, and flower about the end of October, at which time all the available inhabitants of the district are summoned to gather the flowers and separate their stamina: they live in the gardens, in temporary sheds made of leaves and twigs, until the picking is over, and sepoys are stationed all round them to prevent any of the saffron being carried off.

WEEAN is a small village situated about 3 miles to the north-east of *Pámpoor*, at the foot of the spur so conspicuous in the distance for the beautiful regularity of its distorted strata; the road to it lies across the plains and is very easy. It contains three mineral springs and one fresh one.

The MINERAL SPRINGS are called *Phúk Nág*, and the strong sulphurous odour serves as a guide to their situation, which is behind the village. The water issues from the base of the southern side of the spur in three places, within few feet of each other; it flows into a small canal, about a foot wide and a foot deep, lined with stone, and containing small fish. The canal conveys it into the enclosure of the *zeárut* of *Mohammed Sháh*—an old wooden building about 30 yards distant. The FRESH SPRING is called the *Kálish Nág;* it issues from the western side of the same spur, and about 60 yards beyond the uppermost of the three mineral springs; the water is received into a reservoir about 10 yards square and a foot deep, lined with stone, and also containing fish; the stream from this reservoir flows southwards, receiving that of the mineral springs as it issues from beneath the western wall of the old *zearat.*

The MINERAL SPRINGS are highly impregnated with iron and sulphur derived from the *pyrites* which abound in the adjoining mountains; their medicinal virtues are very considerable, and they are highly recommended, both for drinking and bathing, in those disorders in which the similar mineral waters of England and the Continent are found so beneficial, especially in cases of chronic rheumatism, obstinate skin diseases, general debility after fevers, bowel complaints, or affections of the liver, also in chronic diseases peculiar to women. It is to be hoped that before long suitable baths and other buildings will be provided for the use of invalids resorting to these waters, which should however only be taken under proper professional guidance.

IRON WORKS exist at *Shar*, a large village about 2 miles south-east of *Weean:* the mines which supply the ore are at the back of the lofty range of mountains to the north of the village, about 3 miles distant, and over steep and rocky ground. Iron is also smelted at *Soap* in the eastern part, and at *Arwan* in the western part, of the valley.

The RUINS AT LADOO may be visited from *Pámpoor*. Ladoo is a large village at the foot of the hills, about a mile to the south of *Shár*, and about 3 miles north of *Lattapoor*, a very small village on the left bank of the river, and about 3½ miles by land from *Pámpoor*. The ruins consists of an old temple standing in the middle of a stone tank at the southern extremity of the village; it resembles that at *Pandritan*, but is not so perfect. A modern Hindoo temple and two *zearats* are also situated near the edge of the tank, about 50 yards to the north.

KARKARPORE is a small village situated on the left bank of the river, about 4 miles by land, and about four hours' journey by boat, above *Pámpoor*. The *Rámchu River* joins the *Jhelam* just below it, and behind it there are some fine shady trees, also two old ruined temples, and a couple of old cemetries.

The TEMPLE AT PAYECH may be visited from *Karkarpore*, the horses being previously sent there by crossing the bridge at *Pámpoor*. *Páyech* is a small village situated at the foot of the western side, and near the southern extremity of the elevated table-land called the *Nonágri Kareewah*. It is 6 miles from *Karkarpoor*, 10 miles from *Pámpoor*, 5 koss from *Shupiyan*, and 4 koss from *Ramoo;* and the roads from *Pámpoor* and *Karkarpore* are smooth, level, and very pretty all the way.

The temple is one of the latest and most interesting relics of the old Hindú age; it is dedicated to *Vishnu* as *Suryea* or the sun god, and the ceiling is radiated so as to represent the sun; it is situated on the southern side of the village, in a small green space—probably the bed of a tank in former times—and surrounded by a few willows. It is 9 feet square and 5½ feet high; there is an opening on each side with the usual trefoil arches; the interior and exterior are ornamented with peculiar carved figures, resembling those at *Pandritan:* it now contains a *lingam*, and is used by Hindús. The *lumbadar*, or head man of the village, *Soobhan Butt*, well remembered *Vigne* in 1865, and pointed out the spot—about 20 yards to the south of the temple—where more than 35 years before he sat and sketched it for his "travels."

In returning from *Páyech* the village of *Kohil* may be visited; it is about a mile to the north-east of *Páyech;* and on its southern side, about 100 yards beyond, a fine spring which issues from the foot of the *Kareewah*, is a small roofless and half buried temple, resembling that in the *Manasbal Lake.*

LATTAPORE is the name of a small village on the right bank of the river, about an hour and a half's journey by boat above *Karkarpore;* it is about 10 miles by land from *Srinagar*, and the ruins at *Ladoo* may be visited from it.

AWANTIPORE or AVANTIPORE—named after King *Avante Verma*—was also once a capital of Kashmir; it is situated on the right bank of the river, about 17 miles by land, and about fifteen hours' journey by water above Srinagar. The city extended to the mountains behind; it was walled, occupied both sides of the river, and when it flourished Kashmir is said to have been inhabited by 3,000,000 of people. The *Ruins of Awantipore* are famous; the principal of them, which is just below the village, consists of a large quadrangle with the remains of surrounding cloisters, and a temple in the centre, like those at *Martand;* the adjoining *ghât* is also strewn with large masses of stone, portions probably of steps and an old embankment. About a quarter of a mile below the village are the remains of two other temples, of one of which the roofless walls are still standing, but the other is now only a heap of huge masses of stones. In 1865 some excavations were, at the suggestion of the late estemed *Bishop Cotton*, undertaken around the principal ruin, which is supposed to have been erected about A. D. 852; further explorations of these and other Kashmir ruins have been more recently made by *Surgeon-Major H. W. Bellew*, C. S. I., the results of which will probably appear in his forthcoming work on "*Kashmir and Yarkand.*"

TRAHAL is a small town situated near the lower end of a narrow valley, about 6 miles to the north-east of *Awantipore*, and contains a famous *zearat*. The valley is traversed by a stream which flows into the *Jhelam* a little above *Awantipore*, and is called the *Pattarkool*; there are some ravines and passes opening into the valley by which the sportsman may ascend the adjacent lofty mountains, which abound with the larger kinds of game.

After passing the small villages of *Thokna* and *Soorsoo* the junction of the *Veshau* with the *Jhelam* is reached on the left bank of the latter, immediately below the large village of *Marhama*, where there is a ferry which is about seven hours' journey by boat above *Awantipore*. The *Veshau* is one of the largest rivers in Kashmir, and is navigable for a few miles from its mouth; it rises from the famous mountain lake, the *Konsa Nag*, on the top of the *Pir Panjal* and above the village of *Sedau*, which is about 5 miles to the south of *Shupiyan*.

Samma Thang, a lofty mound or conical hill near the left bank of the river, is the mount on which *Kashuf* or *Kusyapa* is supposed to have passed a thousand years in religious abstraction, previous to the desication of the valley: it is the site of an old temple.

Bijbehara or *Vidyea Vihar*, the temple of wisdom, is a large and dilapidated town, built chiefly on the left bank of the river, which is here crossed by a fine old wooden bridge; it is about 9 miles by land above *Awantipore;* the journey by boat occupies about ten hours. One of the oldest and finest temples in Kashmir stood here; it was thrown down by *Sikander*, who built a mosque out of its ruins; *Golab Singh* threw down this mosque, and used the ruins for a new temple. The original temple was built by *Asoka* B. C. 250, and its floor in 1865 was about 14 feet below the level of the surrounding ground.

The remains of an *old pleasure garden* also exist above the town; it was planted on both sides of the river, and the two portions now overshadowed by poplars and magnificent *chénars* were united by a *stone bridge*, the ruins of which may still be seen; that portion on the left bank contains a new *Hindú temple*, that on the right a new *Royal Lodge* for the use of the Maharajah.

Above *Bijbehara* the river gradually diminishes in breadth and depth, while its banks become higher. The

Liddar River joins the right bank in two streams within a mile or two of *Kanbal*, and each is nearly as large as the *Jhelam* itself.

KANBAL is a very small village on the right bank of the river, about 4 miles by land above *Bijbehara*; but the journey by boat occupies about 3½ hours. The river is crossed by a wooden bridge, and boats do not usually ascend beyond it, on account of the shallowness of the water; visitors intending, therefore, to continue their tour in this part of the valley, will here discharge them before proceeding to *Islámabád*, which is about a mile distant. Coolies are usually in waiting at *Kanbal*, but it is safer to send on a messenger the day before, so that they may be in readiness on arrival.

KORWINEE is a small village on the *Veshau*, about 2 or 3 miles south-west of *Kanbal*, and where, as at many other places on this river, there is very good fishing.

ISLAMABAD—the ancient *Anat Nag*—was once a large city, but is now a comparatively small town, containing probably about 1,000 houses. It is situated about a mile from the *Kanbal Bridge*, and under the western side of an elevated table-land or *Wudir* 6 miles long and of the same breadth, upon the edge of which is a conical hill overlooking the town, and commanding a magnificent view of this part of the valley; it is embedded in magnificent chenar, poplar, walnut, pear and other trees, many of which are profusely entwined with the wild vine and other creepers, and it is surrounded by some fine orchards. It contains a famous *zearat*, a Hindú temple, a small pleasure garden, called the *Sirkari Bag*, which is used by the Maharajah and his family when they visit the town, and several springs, which issue from the foot of the *kareewah*. The principal of these are the *Anat Nag*, the *Sonar Pokri*, the *Salik Nag*, and the *Malik Nag*. The *Anat Nag*, the principal one, is close to the *Sirkari Bag*, and is surrounded by a high wall which encloses a space about 70 yards square; the water issues mainly from the foot of the hill and flows through a series of tanks and canals to the outside of the enclosure, where it falls to the ground in a fine cascade about 7 feet high and 7 feet wide. The tanks are about 3 feet deep, and, like the canals, lined with stone and filled with tame fish (Himalayan *trout*), which are regularly fed by the Hindús, who consider them very sacred. There are several pavilions inside the enclosure, one of which is for the use of visitors; the others being reserved for the Maharajah and the attendant priests. The *Sonar Pokri* is situated about 100 yards to the east of the *Anat Nag*; the water is received into a stone tank about 30 feet square, and surrounded by a wall; it is highly esteemed far drinking purposes, and is conveyed to many parts of the town by aqueducts mostly lined with stone. The *Salik Nag* and *Malik Nag* flow into the same tank, which is on the right hand side of the road, *Sonar Pokri ;* the *Salik* issues from a horizontal fissure, and is pure and fresh, while the *Malik* bubbles up in the form of a fountain, and is sulphurous. On the *Banihal* side of the town there is a fine avenue of poplars about half a mile long.

Table of Distances, &c., from Islámabád to places in its vicinity.

FROM	TO	Distance, miles.	Cooly rates.
Islámabád ...	Kanbal	1¼	1 anna.
Ditto	Ruins of Martand ...	4½	2 annas.
Ditto	Bawun	5	2 "
Ditto	Caves of Bhoomjoo ...	6	2 "
Ditto	Atchibal	6	2 "
Ditto	Vernag	17	4 "
Ditto	Nowboog	14	4 "
Ditto	Saogam	10	4 "
Ditto	Kookar Nag	14	4 "

The celebrated RUINS OF MARTAND are situated on the top of the *kareewah*, near the foot of the mountains, and about 5 miles to the north of *Islámabád.* They are the remains of a temple called by the natives *Pándu Larri or Pándu Koru.* Vigne* thus refers to it:—" As an insolated ruin, this deserves, on account of its solitary and massive grandeur, to be ranked, not only as the first ruin of the kind in Kashmir, but as one of the noblest amongst the architectural relics of antiquity that are to be seen in any country." *Martand* means the sun, and the temple was dedicated to his worship, though the first worship of the valley was that of *nag* or snakes. It was probably erected between A.D. 370 and 500, and consists of a massive entrance leading into a large quadrangle, which is surrounded by a fine collonade of fluted pillars with intervening trefoiled recesses, and contains in the centre a lofty edifice, having on each side of it a small and detached wing. The whole ruin is composed of immense masses of stone, and the means by which they were raised to their present positions is still a problem to be solved. It bears marks of *Bactrian* architecture, what Cunningham calls the *Aryan* order; it overlooks one of the finest views in Kashmir, and its site has been compared to that of the *Escorial.* The destroying hand of time is rapidly levelling this ruin, as well as those at *Awantipore* and other places in

* Vigne's "Travels in Kashmir," Vol, I., p. 360.

Kashmir; indeed the process of demolition has been considerable even during the past 10 years, and it is a matter for regret that no efforts are apparently made towards their careful preservation.

BAWAN or MATTAN is a small village containing a very sacred spring: it is about a mile and a half from the ruins of *Martand*, and situated under the northern side of the *kareewah* of *Islámabád*, from whence, by the direct road, it is about 5 miles distant; on the way may be seen, on the right, and deposited in horizontal layers upon the distorted limestone strata, masses of shingly conglomerate, the remains of beaches—witnesses to the former lacustrine state of the Kashmir valley. The spring issues from a horizontal fissure at the foot of the hills behind the village, and is much larger than that of *Anat Nag;* the water is conveyed by a series of tanks and canals to a fine old grove of *chénars* outside the enclosure, from whence it falls into a brook about 15 feet below. The tanks and canals are lined with stone, and the water is crowded with sacred fish, which are regularly fed by the Hindú priests. The spring is sacred to *Vishnu,* who, according to the *Shastras*, divided the mountains at *Baramula,* and thus drained the valley; it is said to have come from the mundane egg breaking in the hand of *Kashuf* after the valley was dried up.

The CAVES of BHOOMJOO or BOOMZOO are places of pilgrimage; they are situated about a mile beyond the village of *Bawan*, and in the mountains which bound the right side of the road leading up the *Liddar Valley*. The two principal ones may be called respectively the *Long Cave* and the *Temple Cave;* the others, of which there are several, are small, mostly near the ground, and were probably made for shelter by *fâkirs* or pilgrims.

The *Long Cave* is the nearest to the village of *Bawan*, from whence the materials for a torch should be taken. The opening is about 40 feet above the ground, and is reached by rough steps worn in the rock; it is ovoid in shape, 6½ feet high, and 3½ feet wide. The Cave is dedicated to *Kaladeva;* it penetrates the mountain in an easterly direction, and may be traversed for about 210 feet; beyond this the passage becomes too small to admit a man, even when crawling, so that its total length cannot be exactly ascertained; the natives, however, believe it to be interminable. It is the abode of numerous bats, and the rock in many places is beautifully honeycombed by the action of water, which is constantly trickling from the higher portion of the roof. About 20 feet from the entrance there is a low and narrow passage leading off to the left; and about 60 feet beyond it, on the same side, is a small and circular chamber, which, when visited by the author, contained the bones of a human skeleton. The following are the dimensions of the accessible portion of this cave :—

			The average width.	The average height.
In the first		... 22 feet	3½ feet.	6½ feet.
In the next		... 24 „	1½ „	5½ „
Ditto	...	... 44 „	4 „	12 „
Ditto	...	... 40 „	13 „	20 „
Ditto	...	... 40 „	9½ „	12 „
Ditto	...	... 40 „	1 foot.	2 „
	Total	... 210 feet.	5½ feet.	9⅔ feet.

The *Temple Cave* is in the same mountain, and about three minutes' walk beyond the *Long Cave* ; its entrance is nearly 100 feet above the ground, and is ornamented by a porch about 10 feet high and 10 feet wide, cut out of the solid rock, and formed with the usual trefoil arch. The interior is oval, about 48 feet long, 27 feet wide, and 13½ feet high ; it contains two platforms, the upper of which supports a Hindú temple built of stone, of pyramidal shape, about 11¼ feet square, and one of the most perfect specimens of this style of architecture to be seen in any part of the country. The Cave is cleanly kept, and its entrance commands a beautful view of the lower portion of the *Liddar Valley*. The *zearat*, which stands a few feet beyond it, is that of *Baba Bamdeen Rishi* ; and the tomb of his disciple, *Rookoodeen Rishi*, is contained in a small but massive chamber close by it. The visitor may now either pursue his journey up the *Liddar Valley* to *Pálgám* and the *Cave of Ambernáth* (described in a subsequent section) or return to *Islámabád* and thence visit the following place :—

ATCHIBAL—famous for its fine springs—is situated at the extremity of the low range of hills which separates the pergunnahs of *Bringh* and *Kotihár*, and is about 6 miles to the east of *Islámabád*, from whence it is visible. The springs are at the upper end of an old pleasure garden, built by the Emperor *Jehángir* ; they are amongst the finest in Kashmir, and are supposed to be the re-appearance of the river *Bringh,* whose waters suddenly disappear through a large fissure in its limestone bed, some miles to the eastward; the water, which is icy-cold, issues from several places near the foot of the low and densely fir-clad spur, welling up in one through an oblique fissure nearly large enough to admit a man's body, and forming, at times, a mound of water some 18 inches high and a foot in diameter. The garden is surrounded by a stone wall, it is arranged in terraces, contains many fruit trees, some very large *chénars,* a *hamám* or bath and several pretty pavilions on the tanks and canals through which the water flows, and which, after serving numerous fountains, leaves the lower part of the garden by three fine waterfalls, the largest of which is about 8 feet high and 16 feet wide. This is a lovely place for a few days encampment; it was a favorite resort of the beautiful *Núrmahal;* there are some very large *chénars* just outside it, and adjoining one of the walls is a new *Royal Lodge*, for the use of the Maharajah and his suite. At the upper end of the garden are some ruined arches, portions of a long and subterranean passage probably.

ATCHIBAL TO VERNAG.—The visitor can proceed either direct or *viâ* the *Nowboog* Valley; in the former case the distance is about 15 miles or one long march; the road lies along the plains, but occasionally across the beds of streams, so that it is as well to halt for a few hours' rest at one of the villages about half-way. The following is the route *via Nowboog* :—

ATCHIBAL TO NOWBOOG.—*Distance* 12 *miles.*

The road turns to the east, passing through *Shángus* about 4 miles off, and formerly celebrated for the number and beauty of its *danseuse*, the family of which appears now extinct. It is an old and dilapidated village, washed on one side by a fine stream of pure cold water, and shaded by some magnificent *chénars;* the low hill close to it commands an extensive view of the *Kotihar* Pergunnah, through which the *Arpat*, one of the head waters of the *Jhelam*, flows towards *Kanbal.* A mile or so beyond *Shángus* is another small village situated near the commencement of the long, narrow, and densely-wooded gullee, through which the path leads over the ridge into the *Nowboog Nai* or Valley, and which is fit for ponies as well as *dandies*. NOWBOOG is a very small village situated at the mouth of a glen which opens into the valley ; there is no bungalow, and provisions and coolies are rather scarce, but there are some lovely spots for encamping. The *Nowboog Valley* is long and narrow, its general direction is nearly north and south, it is bounded on each side by lofty pine-clad mountains, its surface is undulating, and the profusion of grass and trees gives it a beautiful park-like appearance: it is about 8 miles long, averages less than 1½ miles in width, and is one of the finest grazing grounds in the country. It is traversed by a stream which rises at its upper end, near the foot of the *Margan Pass*, which is 11,600 feet high, and leads over the mountains into the *Wardwan Valley*, and flows into the River *Bringh* at its lower end, where it opens into the pergunnah of that name. The climate of the valley is delicious ; the neighbouring mountains abound with bears and other animals, so that it is a very favorite place with sportsmen ; its exquisite scenery makes it equally so to ordinary visitors, who are in the habit of resorting to it as an agreeable change from Srinagar during the hot and unhealthy months.

NOWBOOG TO KOOKAR NAG.—*Distance* 12 *miles.*

There are two roads—a short one over the range of hills by the village of *Soap*, and a long one passing round the same range by the bridge of *Tansan*. The first is steep and rough, about 7 miles long, and only fit for coolies; the other is tolerably level, easy, and very pretty; it leads down the *Nowboog Valley* and, turning to the right, opens into the *Bringh Valley* by the *Tansan* bridge, which is about 7 miles from *Nowboog* and overlooked by the *Masjid* of *Hajee Daud Sahib*, picturesquely situated on the hill side; after crossing the bridge it joins the high road from *Kashmir* to *Kishtwar*. KOOKAR NAG is about 5 miles to the north-west of the *Tansan* birdge, and about 8 miles to the south-east of *Atchibal;* it consists of a collection of springs situated at the foot of a long range of verdant hills on the left, near the small village of *Hargamoo,* and which separates the pergunnah of *Bringh* from that of *Shahabad*. The water is very cold, and so celebrated for its purity that the Pathan Governors are said to have been supplied with it; it issues from about six places close to each other, and only a few feet from the base of the hills, which are covered by low jungle. The stream, which is formed, is about 12 feet wide, and flows in a north-westerly direction to join the *Bringh.*

Soap or *Soofahan* is a small village situated on the side of the bare and rugged mountains on the right bank of the *Bringh*, nearly opposite to, and about 2½ miles from, *Kookar Nág*; it is worthy of notice as one of the few places in which iron-works exist. The ore is obtained from the neighbouring hills, which are also said to contain veins of lead, copper, silver, and even veins of gold: iron, however, is the only metal at present worked in Kashmir.

KOOKAR NAG TO VERNAG.—*Distance 7½ miles.*

Vernág is situated in the *Shahabad Valley*, and on the other side of the *Kookar Nág* range of hills; the road continues for a short distance along the foot of the hills, then turns up a broad defile on the left, and ascends by a smooth and easy path to the village of *Noroo*, about a mile and a half from *Kookar Nág*. There are two roads from *Noroo* to *Vernág*—a short, and rough one *viâ Buttgoond*, fit for coolies; and a rather longer but easier one *viâ Shahabad*, by which the distance from *Kookar Nág* to *Vernág* is about 7 or 8 miles. *Shahabad* is within about 3 miles of *Vernág*; it was once a royal town, and the largest at the eastern end of the valley, but is now a ruined village and unworthy of a special visit.

VERNAG is the most famous spring in Kashmir, and the acknowledged source of the *Jhelam*; it is situated at the foot of the mountains and close to the *Banihál Pass.* Around it are the ruins of an old pleasure garden built by the Emperor *Jehangir* between A.D. 1612, and 1619, and the buildings, aqueducts, and fountains are said to have been chiefly designed by his lovely and devoted wife *Núr Mehal,* otherwise called *Núr Jehán,* or the light of the world; the water of the spring, which is very cold and of a deep bluish-green color, is received into an octagonal stone basin about 111 feet wide, 50 feet deep in the centre, 10 feet deep at the sides, and filled with sacred fish; after flowing through the garden in stone-lined canals it shortly joins the *Sandrahán.* Around the basin is an old building consisting of 24 arched alcoves, which were faced with large and elaborately carved stones, many of which still remain: upon one of these is a Persian inscription giving the date and name of the Emperor by whose order the building was constructed. This was the favorite place of *Jehangir,* and whither he desired to be carried in his last moments, as previously mentioned. Sir Henry Lawrence once pitched his tent here for some time; and in 1856 General Nicholson was encamped here for about six weeks.

The visitor may now return to *Srinagar,* either by *water* from the *Kanbal* pier near *Islámabád,* about 16 miles distant, or by *land* along the southern side of the valley, where there are several glens and minor valleys lying just within the neighbouring mountains, resembling that of *Nowboog*, and equally suitable for change of air and scene. This route is as follows:—

VERNAG TO THE ROZLOO.—*Distance* 8 *miles.*

The road passes in a north-westerly direction, close under the low and verdant hills which lie at the foot of the *Pir Panjal* mountains, and is tolerably smooth and level all the way. VATERITTER is a collection of springs like those of *Kookar Nág:* they are considered by some as the true source of the *Jhelam*, and are situated on the side of the road, about 200 yards beyond the village of *Gutalgund*, which is about a mile from *Vernág*. The water issues from three principal places within a few feet of each other, and about 100 feet from the northern side of the hills. The ROZLOO VALLEY is situated within the hills, at the foot of the *Pir Panjal*, and may be reached either by a foot-path or by a bridle-path. The former leads through an opening in the hills on the left of the road, and about five minutes' walk beyond the village of *Tanjool;* it passes through a beautiful park-like scenery, and after a gradual ascent of about a mile and half, conducts to the foot of a low ridge, the summit of which commands a fine view of the valley; the bridle-path leads up a long defile to the left, near the village of *Yor.* The ROZLOO VALLEY is oval in shape, about 3 miles long and 2 miles broad, and contains about a dozen villages; it is surrounded by hills, and bounded on the south by the grassy slopes of the snow-capped *Pir Panjal;* the scenery is exceedingly pretty, the soil is very rich, and its climate enjoys a high reputation. From the top of the ridge, above the village of *Rozloo*, a view may be obtained of another small valley, called *Bringhin Lannor*, the names of two villages which it contains. These valleys were formerly very famous for their grapes, which yielded the best wine in Kashmir.

ROZLOO VALLEY TO BAN DOOSAR.—*Distance* 10½ *miles.*

The *road* is tolerably smooth and easy, passes mostly along the foot of the low hills under the *Pir Panjal*, through very fine scenery all the way, and opens into the plains near the village of *Yor;* turning to the left, it then leads to the village of *Charat*, about 1½ miles further on, and after passing over some undulating ground, conducts to the large village of *Saogám*, about 4 miles from *Rozloo*, and about 10 milee from *Islámabád.* About 3 miles further on, the village of *Pet Doosar* is seen a few yards to the right, prettily situated in the midst of fine *chenárs*; just beyond it the road descends, and continues to *Bán Doosar*, which is a small village about 4 miles further on, lying under the range of low hills on the left, and on the bank of a cool and clear stream which flows in front of it. There is no bungalow, and supplies are not abundant, but there are some very pleasant spots for encampment.

BAN DOOSAR TO NOHÁN.—*Distance* 10½ *miles.*

The first two miles of the road are smooth and level; it then crosses the stony bed of the *Veshau* by a ford, and thence continues all the way along the left bank of this river, being tolerably level, but generally rough with large round stones; several small streams also have to be forded, so that altogether this is rather a fatiguing march. KOOLGAM is a small town about 3 miles from *Bán Doosar*, very picturesquely situated on the southern side of a *kareewah*, and overlooking the *Veshau*; it contains two old *zearats*; the larger one is that of *Hussain Simnáree*, and the smaller one that of *Shah Hamadán*. KOL NARAWAH is a valley or strath about 10 miles long, from 1½ to 2 miles broad, and opens into the plains on the right bank of the *Veshau*, near the village of *Kúri*. It contains about half a dozen villages, the principal of which is *Hanjipoor*, prettily situated on the hill side at the upper end of the strath: it is a capital place for a few days' ramble.

From KOOLGAM the road shortly descends again to the level of the *Veshau*, and passes to NOHAN, which is a small village within a few yards of the left bank of the river. There is no bungalow, and provisions are not abundant, but there are some trees near it suitable for encampment. Just beyond *Kúri*, on the opposite side of the river, and on a small hill, is the *zearat* of *Baba Kaim-u-deen* standing in the midst of a forest.

NOHAN TO SHUPIYAN.—There are two roads, a direct one about 9 miles long, and another by the village of *Sedau*, which is about 13½ miles; they are both tolerably level, smooth and easy: the servants and baggage may be sent by the former, while the visitor proceeds by the latter to see the cataract of *Haribal.* The first two miles of this road are rough, like the previous march; it then opens into a fine grassy plain, and shortly ascends a table-land to the village of *Rishinagar*, which is small but surrounded by some large *chenárs;* thence it shortly descends, and continues for about three miles along the left bank of the river to the mouth of the gorge, through which it issues from the mountains. The *Veshau*—one of the largest rivers in Kashmir—rises from the *Kónsa Nág*, a fine mountain-lake about half a mile long, somewhat more than a quarter of a mile wide, and situated on the top of the *Pir Panjál*, at an elevation of about 13,000 feet. The water leaves the lake through an irregular rocky opening in its western side, and falls into a long, deep, and narrow gorge, by which it is conducted down to the plains of Kashmir. This gorge, especially its lower portion, is simply a channel through the hard and solid rocks, the strata of which lie obliquely across the course of the torrent; in several parts of it there are high ledges and rocky walls, over which the river dashes in splendid waterfalls, like some of those in Switzerland, and on some of the American rivers. HARIBAL is one of these, and in the early part of the season, when the snows are melting, it is a magnificent cataract—the finest in Kashmir. It is situated about a quarter of a mile within the mouth of the gorge, and may best be viewed from the top of a lofty precipice overhanging the left bank of the torrent, which may be reached by a steep path turning off to the left of the road leading up the gorge to the *Sedau Pass* and the *Kónsa Nág.* This spot is said to have been the last resting place for the feet of many a Hindú fanatic; and a more certain death than a leap from it into the rocky abyss below, can scarcely be conceived. *Sedau* is a very pretty village situated upon an eminence about a mile to the north of the *Veshau* gorge, from whence, however, it cannot be seen, as it is hidden by an intervening range of low and wooded hills; it is about 8 miles from *Nohán*, 5 from *Shupiyan*, and about 5 from

Hirpoor. SHUPIYAN is the largest town on the southern side of the valley, and is situated on the high road between *Bhimber* and *Srinagar.* The bungalows for visitors are at the southern end of the town, and supplies of all the kinds are usually abundant.

SHUPIYAN TO RAMOO AND CHRAR.—The distance to *Rámoo* is about 10 miles, and the road is described in Chapter II.

CHRAR is about 3½ miles from *Rámoo*, and contains the *zearat* of the celebrated Mahomedan Saint *Shah Núr-ú-din.* The road is smooth and white, and passes to the west, over three or four *kareewahs,* across the intervening valleys, and amidst beautiful scenery all the way. CHRAR is a large and well-built town, snugly situated in a recess upon the side of a high and naked table-land, overlooking a broad and deep ravine, and commanding an extensive prospect. The shrine is situated on the northern side of a hill above the town, and is surrounded by a substantial brick wall, on the inner side of which are wooden shades for the use of the pilgrims. The building is of the usual kind, and resembles the *Shah Hamadán* in Srinagar; it is, however, the most sacred and frequented *zearat* in Kashmir, and although there is no bungalow for visitors, supplies are abundant, and there are several places suitable for encampment.

CHRÁR TO SRINAGAR.—*Distance* 15 *miles.*

The road passes down the ravine opposite the town, and then through a long and narrow valley; after a while it ascends the range on the left, and passes through a gap which is about 3 miles from *Chrár;* it then leads along a *kareewah* which commands one of the most extensive views of the valley anywhere to be obtained. *Nilnág* is about a quarter of a mile from the gap, and is an oval piece of water lying in a deep hollow on the left of the road, about 100 yards long and 20 yards wide; the water is derived from springs, and the place is considered very holy by the Hindús. Colored woollen socks and gloves of a very superior kind are manufactured at *Wahtor*, a large village about 8 miles from *Chrár*, and upon the high road from *Shupiyan* to Srinagar which has been previously described in Chapter III.

THE LIDDAR VALLEY.

The LIDDAR VALLEY opens into the North-eastern corner of the Kashmir Valley, and gives passage to the river of the same name; it is about 26 miles long, and extends in a north-easterly direction from near *Islámabád* to about a mile above *Palgam*, where it divides into two defiles which stretch obliquely—one towards the north-west, and leading to the *Sind Valley*, the other towards the north-east, and leading up to the *Sheesha Nag* and the sacred *Cave of Ambernáth*. At its lower end it is 3 or 4 miles wide, but at its upper end it is only a few hundred yards; it is bounded on both sides by mountains, which are increasingly lofty, especially in its upper half; they are covered with dense forest and jungle, and are favorite haunts of the *barah singa*, *markhor*, and other animals interesting to the sportsman.

The LIDDAR RIVER separates the pergunnahs of *Kaurpára* on its left bank from that of *Dachinpára*—famous for its fine breed of ponies—on its right. It is next in size to the *Sind River*, and is formed a few hundred yards below the village of *Palgam*, by the junction of the two streams which flow through the defiles at the head of the valley, that on the right flows from the *Sheesha Nag*, and may be regarded as its source; it is a rapid and unnavigable torrent, and its bed is very rough throughout nearly the whole of its course.

THE CAVE OF AMBERNATH

Is a place of pilgrimage sacred to *Siva* (who is said to have assumed the form of a block of ice and taken up his abode there), and is celebrated throughout India as well as Kashmir, being to the Hindus what *Mecca* is to the Moslems; it is annually visited by thousands of people (male and female), who wend their way to the religious festival which takes place there about the end of July.

It is situated in the distant snowy mountains far away from all human habitation, and even above the region of vegetation, being at an elevation of more than 16,000 feet above the sea. The road leads up the *Liddar* Valley, and beyond *Pálgám* some portions of it are not only difficult but dangerous, from occasional sudden landslips or rolling avalanches, so that serious, and often fatal, accidents are of almost annual occurrence; those who perish thus are, however, esteemed fortunate, and their end felicitous. Several ladies have of late safely and successfully accomplished the journey, a feat as courageous, or even more so, than that of many an *Alpine* mountaineer, and one to talk about, with no less pride, in after years.

The pilgrims halt at *Islámabád* to lay in their stock of provisions, for little or nothing is procurable along the road; and thence they march to the Cave in groups, and by the following stages:—

Pilgrim Route from Islámabád to the Cave of Ambernáth.

No.	Names of stages.	Distance, miles.	REMARKS.
	From Islámabád ...		A good baraduree.
1	To Eishmakam ...	12½	An encamping ground.
2	Pálgám ...	14	Ditto.
3	Tánin ...	10	Ditto.
4	Sheesha Nag ...	10	Ditto.
5	Panjtarni ...	10	Ditto.
6	Ambernáth ...	4½	Ditto.

An admirable account of a journey to this Cave was published in the *Pioneer* of the 15th March, 1867, by the well-known H. C. C.,* and as it is sure to prove interesting, especially to his brother sportsmen, it is given nearly *in extenso;* the several places named will be found on the accompanying map.

"I went by boat from Srinagar as far as Islámabád on the 1*st* and 2*nd August.* The temperature of the air was 76°, and the water 68 at the latter place, being respectively 6° below that of the former. There is a large *barah-dari* (summer-house) overlooking some reservoirs filled with fish, shaded by fine chenar (plane) trees. There are also a private residence and garden of the Maharajah's. At the back of the village rises a ridge, from which the windings of the Jhelam and a general *coup d'œil* of the valley appear to advantage. *Mártand* and *Atchibal* are neighbouring "lions" generally visited. No works of art, however, can compete with nature. Her admirers are strongly recommended to go up the *Liddar* Valley, to *Pylgam* and *Aro.* It is a gentlemanly or rather lady-like trip, and does not *require a 'muscular Christian' to perform it.* I had started from

* The late Lieutenant-Colonel H. C. Cuppage, B.S.C. who committed suicide on the 18th September 1872, whilst labouring under temporary insanity, by laying himself on the rails of the *Ulster* Railway at *Lurgan;* a train from *Dublin* passed over the body and completely severed the head from the trunk. Many will regret the sad fate of this amiable and accomplished officer; he was one of the best shots in the Indian army.

Srinagar with the intention of proceeding alone, but was so fortunate as to induce two friends of the 35th Regiment, whom I met on the river, to join me.

"4th.—*Pauzgam*, 12 miles, 1 mile from *Sullur*. The usual encamping place is *Eishmakám*, on the high road to the right, 2 miles back. The river consists of a network of channels, rapid, clear, and running over a stony bed. I should say it would repay the fisherman to pitch his tent anywhere hereabouts for several days, but the paddy-fields and mosquitoes which they breed are a nuisance. Quantities of fruit all along—walnuts, apples, plums, mulberries, &c. Thermometer 80° at 5 P. M.

"5th.—*Pylgam* 12 miles. Latter half of the road lovely. The valley is two miles broad, cultivated, and with wooded (pine) and grassy plateaus above, at the back of which abruptly rise high walls of rock. The village is pleasantly situated between two defiles, the road to *Kolahoi* and the *Harbagwan glacier* north, and that to *Ambernáth* east. Due south are some fine snow-peaks. Rain.

"6th.—*Tanin*, 10 miles. Rode part of the way and sent back the pony, as it became stony. (Subsequently I found this was a mistake—could have taken him all the way.) Grand scenery, high cliffs, grassy or wooded slopes (*abies* and *picea*, with juniper above). Encamped on a grass plain. Found the sun hot. Have left the flies and musquitoes behind. Very heavy shower at night. Cliffs frequented by ibex in spring.

"7th.—*Zoijpal*, 9 miles, 1 from *Sheesha Nag*. In the first half of the road we ascended 1,000 feet or so, and lost sight of the river, though we saw some cascades which fall into it, which hitherto was a confined torrent, occasionally issuing from snow-beds. A grass plain again, with large detached rocks, which sheltered us from rain. Cold and uncomfortable till we got our tents up, firewood scarce, consisting of merely a few stunted shrubs on a precipitous range.

"8th.—*Wawajan*, 4 miles. Rained all the way. Encamped on a grass plain with only one rock, which afforded poor shelter to the coolies. Passed *Sheesha Nag*, or the glassy or leaden lake, which is 'about one-third of a mile in diameter, lying chiefly in a punch-bowl, formed by nearly perpendicular precipices of a limestone ridge, whose strata up to the summits were twisted and distorted.' In the evening I knocked about the valley, trying to shoot marmots; they are pretty practice for the rifle, but take a great deal of killing, and generally get away into their holes wounded. Their fur is long but coarse. From above the lake the view is very grand. *Panjtarni*, 1,600 feet high at the head of the valley, a semi-circular, brown perpendicular wall with snow patches, and the glacier at the head of the lake, from which rises the 'leaden' peak, 1,700 feet high, a mass of virgin snow.

"9th.—*Googam*, 12 miles, (none of these places are villages,) the junction of the *Ambernáth* and *Sind River*, which flows into the *Jhelum* near *Srinagar*. Breakfasted at *Panjtarni* Valley, near which are a series of very picturesque glaciers, and perpendicular black strata ribbed with snow, sandstone, and shingle. No firewood along this march, except a few juniper bushes.

"10*th.*—Visited *Ambernáth Cave*, 3 miles north-east. A 'burster' of 500 feet at starting, afterwards a gradual ascent up the river over snow the greater part of the way. On approaching, the cave has a square appearance. I judged it to be about 50 yards long, 50 broad at mouth, 30 at the centre, and 30 to 35 high, which dimensions are very much larger than those given by Vigne. It is of gypsum. There are blocks of ice in clefts in the rock, which are probably frozen springs. They never melt, and, as I imagine, their size and permanence are regulated by the strength of the springs. We thought it no desecration to chip off some bits to cool our brandy-and-water at luncheon. If any of us swallowed Siva, we felt no ill effects from it! I was disappointed with the cave *per se*, but the concomitant scenery is of Titanic splendour: a noble glacier, and red sandstone serrated cliffs 1,000 feet high, on either side of the defile. A huge 'black serpent' is said by the priests to inhabit the cave, but we did not find him at home. I was not sorry to turn my back on a place which, from its dreariness, created a feeling of depression difficult to shake off.

"'Here never shines the sun, here nothing breeds,
Unless the nightly owl or fatal raven.
And, when they showed me this abhorred pit,
They told me, here, at dead hour of the night,
A thousand fiends, a thousand hissing snakes,
Ten thousand swelling toads, as many urchins,
Would make such fearful and confused cries,
As any mortal body hearing it,
Should straight fall mad, or else die suddenly.'

"I should say the high cliffs are frequented by ibex; indeed, we saw one, and picked up a horn 42 inches in length, and next day observed a large herd of does on a continuation of the same range. Markham, in his book, mentions having seen a variety of 'wild sheep' in this district. I cannot imagine what they were, unless they were shápoo or ooreál (*O. Vignii,*) which had wandered over from Ladák. All animals of the *Ovine* and *Caprine* genus do wander from their proper localities occasionally. Burhal have been shot at the Pinduree Glacier, near Almorah, and a thar was killed in the Nowboog ravine last year.

"11*th.*—*Astun Murg*, 10 or 12 miles. My two friends started for *Baltal* in the *Sind Valley*, going down the *Sangamkol River*, as their leave was approaching termination. The road they afterwards found not open. A few miles from *Googam* I crossed a snow-pass, on arriving at which I saw extended before and around me an enormous expanse of snow, bounded by bare limestone mountains. Over this I trudged, ascending a ridge forming the eastern boundary of *Rub Murg*. A snow-storm came on, and my *soi disant* guide informed me that the direction of the onward road puzzled him. This was a pleasant predicament to be in! I then with difficulty retraced my steps, and got down to where I should find firewood, none of which we had seen for ten miles. Encamped in an exceedingly romantically situated glen where there is a natural forest of birch trees, in the evening I knocked over a hind bara-singh across the river, at the long distance of 350 yards, with a hexagonal loaded shell. She rolled down about 150 feet, and I thought would never rise again. My man, however, on going to the place, merely found a pool of blood! She had got away into dense forest, and I was disappointed in a venison steak for dinner.

"12*th.*—Sunday. Halt. The two Ts. to breakfast, having been obliged to turn within two miles of their goal from the road being so precipitous; the usual route is down and on the river over snow, but the snow had burst or disappeared in several places. They then went on towards *Pálgam*. The previous day, as I was coming along, I saw high up above us on the mountain side, which was covered with deep snow, a herd of ten or twelve ponies; what they were doing there I could not say. To-day they were again seen, standing disconsolate, looking in the same place. I should say the poor animals must ultimately have all perished. Isolated pillars of rock on the mountain ridges occur hereabouts, and are good landmarks. Rain for three days in the day time; mornings and evenings fine. Saw a moonal pheasant, the first game-bird since I left.

"14*th*.—*Rub Murg*. Encamped by a small lake always containing masses of floating snow when not frozen over. There is a legend that the "fairies" bathe in it. *Rub Murg* is an extensive triangular plain, with slate, limestone, and shingle ridges on three sides. Waiting for the coolies to come up, I was examining the ground through a telescope, when I discovered a herd of eight male and eleven female ibex, feeding within 500 or 600 yards. Desiring my people to keep quiet and pitch camp in a hollow, I went after them at 12 o'clock, and returned at 5 P.M., after having been amongst the herd for two hours, during which time I was unable to distinguish them, although we heard the stones rattling under their feet, from a severe hail and snow-storm and mist. Notwithstanding the elevation and snow, I counted thirty different flowers to-day on one hill.

"15*th.*—Lay in bed during the morning, whilst a glorious sun was drying the wet things of yesterday. Tent like a board from frost during the night, and hail and snow all round 6 inches deep, giving the appearance of winter. The ibex being visible after breakfast near the same spot, I was enticed out, and toiled after them for six hours, at an elevation of 15,000 or 16,000 feet, chiefly along the ridge, where I commanded either side, without coming across them. Some ugly ground, where, if one missed his footing, he would be precipitated 2,000 feet. The grass was so scarce, the ibex were on the move all day, feeding; hence my missing them. From such an elevation I had a good view of the *Gwashbrari* or *Kolahoi* Peak (17,839 feet high), and the surrounding glaciers. Camp probably 14,500 feet.

"16*th.*—Marched at 7 A.M., going over deep snow, which, however, was frozen crisp. Encamped in *Harbagwan,* by the lake *Har Nág,* which is about two miles in circumference. The banks on two sides rise gradually and are bare. *Harbagwan* is an undulating grassy plain, depasturing many ponies and immense herds of sheep. Coming along, I came upon a herd of ibex (females), at which I had four shots from my Beasley, and one from my Lancaster rifle, at 50 to 130 yards, all of which were hits. Bagged two, and lost a third, which had a forearm broken. She was a fine old doe, with horns of 16 inches, being the longest I have ever heard of, with the exception of a pair Mr. Brinkman got, which measured 19 inches.

"17*th*.—Three miles short of *Buj Murg*, 8 miles. This place is not marked on the map, but it is about half-way to *Aro*. After crossing the ridge at the head of *Har Nág*, the road lies down a branch of the *Aro* River. I had the alternative of going to *Kolahoi* by skirting the *Gwashbrari* glaciers due north, but foolishly followed the suggestion of my guide, who said he would show me stags at *Buj Murg*. I was too early for them there, as it turned out. But I was not sorry at having seen such a beautiful part of *Dachinpára*. I made an easy march on the 18th to *Buj Murg*. The scenery on the 17th was very varied, being made up of glens delightfully wooded with sycamore, birch, willows, roses, &c., grassy glades, glaciers, and snow-peaks, high precipitous crags, and detached rocks. At *Buj Murg* it was entirely altered, having softened down into rounded grassy hills and pine-clad dells. We had one ascent (leaving the river) of about 1,000 feet through forest. Shot a fine lamergeyer, 8 feet expanse of wings, and 4 feet long, and saw two black bears. On the plateau of *Buj Murg* there are several ponds, which were much frequented by does and fawns. Later in the season I should think it would be an admirable head-quarters for stag-shooting. There is a clump of pine and birch trees to encamp in; the ground is easy, and supplies can be obtained from *Pálgám*, only 4 miles off.

"20*th.*—*Aro*—5 miles—a steep, disagreeable descent down a *khud*, through heavy, wet, and high jungle. The district of *Aro* is famous for stags in the season, also ibex in spring. There are only two houses. A painter might make a series of pictures here. The best view is from the *Kolahoi* road. An extensive grassy plateau is spread out before you, with the hamlet of *Aro* in the centre; the *Liddar* River glistens in the sunshine as it winds through deep pine-clad ravines; the primeval forests beyond form a crescent, and in the distance appear eternal snow-peaks and a glacier.

"21*st.*—*Kolahoi*, 12 miles. Breakfasted in forest at *Lidarwat*—famous for its ibex cliffs. The first part of the road good and rideable; the latter rough, a pony requiring to be led over the rocks. Glorious cloudless morning; rain in the afternoon. *Kolahoi* is a grass valley lying north and east, it is about 4 miles in length, and at its head is a magnificent glacier. *En route* is a pretty waterfall. To see the former to advantage you ought to overlook it by ascent either right or left. The former is easier, there being a path at the bottom of the glacier. Were the latter, however, ascended, the glaciers on the other side of the watershed, the *Sind Valley*, *Lar Pargannah*, &c., would also be visible. From what I know of the country, it would be one of the most glorious views obtainable in Kashmir. The peak of *Harbagwan* is marked 16,055 feet on the map. For one roughing it, I can recommend a rock at the base of the glacier for shelter. It is about 30 yards square, and has extensive chambers all round. To these bears resort in winter. I remained a week in the valley, trying both north, south, east, and west, for bara-singh. The day after my arrival, encamping to the left, I had the river bridged, as I depended chiefly on the mountain to the right. On the third day a cooly saw a stag, and on the morning of the 4th my scouts reported some ibex high up among the cliffs due west. I did not see them myself, but a magnificent stag came from the same place, passed within 400 yards of my tent, and crossed the river. At the same time I observed two more due east, at the head of the ravine, on a snow bed. I knew this ground well, having on a former occasion knocked over a couple of stags there; so as they seemed disposed to remain there some time, I thought I should be able to find them next morning. That night I moved up from the southern to the northern part of the valley, and slept under the rock, by which move, I thought I should circumvent them. Ascended the mountain the following morning 2,000 or 3,000 feet and got to the place where the stags were last seen. Not, however, finding them, we examined the snow bed and discovered they had gone down it. Tracked over the snow and through forest for three miles, when the marks leading up again I gave up the chase, returning to camp. These were all that were seen. I had a little difficulty about coolies here, from discharging the old batch on arrival. The *mela* was going on at the Cave, and not a man was to be had from south. I, however, had some nine shepherds seized, as they slept in their tents at night, from a place five or six miles off. I say 'seized,' as they would have run away on a requisition being made. Once in camp, they became quite reconciled, taking it as a matter of course; stayed several days, and proved a good lot. During my stay at *Kolahoi* there was slight rain every day.

"28*th.*—*Lidurwut.*

"29*th.*—Ten miles, two beyond the pass at the head of *Tar Sar Lake*, in which I bathed. The water was not as cold as I should have fancied, considering the altitude. To the westward are several other lakes or tarns. They are all surrounded by bare, barren mountains; the water is deep-blue and clear. The group to the south of *Jaji*

Murg are called *Sona* (the golden), *Chanda* (the silver), *Mar Sar*, &c. They contain no fish, and wild-fowl rarely settle on them. The wood to-day consisted entirely of birch. Towards Nagbanan (good stag ground)—a pretty green valley—pines again commence. Met Mr. B., (19th Hussars,) who had been through Ladák, about which country his and his former companion's (Mr. K's) exploits there we had a talk. They had come across and captured specimens of a new animal—a jet-black wolf.

"30*th*.—*Sootoor* village, 9 miles. Crossed the *Tamnag* Range. In the vicinity of *Tar Sar* are immense masses of stones, which in former times came down from the mountains above, or else cropped out of the ground. These are ugly places to lead a pony over; indeed, he requires to be sure-footed and active, not to come to grief. The descent down the spur to *Sootoor* is not rideable. Passed an exceedingly pretty *Pândú Temple* imbedded in jungle.

"31*st*—Five miles. Ascent of 1,000 feet or so over the *Westarwan* Ridge to *Krew*. A grass plain with a tank, orchard, and chénár trees by a largish village. A capital place for chikore-shooting under the hills. Made a nice little bag, which, however, would have been much heavier had I had retrievers; many wounded birds getting away.

"*1st September.*—Ten or twelve miles into Srinagar, having been out exactly a month, during which I enjoyed myself much despite the rain, which always falls in August. Some of the lakes, the cave, "murgs" or valleys, and glaciers, I saw are of a peculiarly impressive character; and now I have given a route which can be traversed by the most delicate, I have no doubt, they will be more generally visited, particularly as they are within an easy distance of the capital. It is to such places that the artist, with camera or palette, ought to direct his steps, there to immortalize his impressions of nature as seen in her most *outré* aspect.

"It may have occurred to the sportsman that I had no shooting. I did not expect it in August. True, after the 20th or so, stag sometimes appear on the grassy slopes and are shot with *perfect* heads though generally in "velvet." As a rule, however, they are very high up among the eternal glaciers and snow, in the ground that ibex frequent in spring. I might have shot bears, but as they were changing their fur, they were not worth firing at. One day a cooly (clever in his way) enticed a she-bear so close up to us by imitating the call of that animal, that I thought it advisable to pelt her with stones, as familiarity might have bred contempt.

In the body of my paper I have mentioned some of the good ibex mountains I have known of a 46-inch head having been shot at *Lidarwat.* Early in the season, I believe, one ought to make a good bag. From the 20th September the whole of the *Dachinpára* district, &c., are renowned for bara-singh.

The Wardwan Valley.

The Wardwan or Maru Wardwan is a long and narrow valley lying on the eastern side of the Kashmir Valley, from which it is separated by a very lofty range of mountains. Its directon is nearly north and south, its length about 40 miles, and its average breadth little more than a quarter of a mile. It is bounded by high and rugged mountains, which are covered with perpetual snow, and which almost entirely exclude the sun from its lower portions; it is intersected by the *Wardwan* River, which rises in the north, flows southward to join the *Chenab,* and receives in its course several tributaries from the numerous minor valleys which open on each side of it, and are called *Nyes.* It is traversed by the road which leads from the province of *Kishtwar* on the south to *Sooroo* and *Kargil* on the north, and thence to *Leh,* the capital, of *Ladák.*—(See No. 23 in Montgomerie's *Kashmir Route Map.*)

It may be reached from *Islamabad* in four marches by two routes; first, by the *Margan Pass* to *Inshin;* and second, by the *Hoksar Pass* to *Maru,* as may be seen in

Nos. 15 and 16 of Montgomerie's *Kashmir Route Map.* There is also a path from *Chittur,* a village at the foot of the hills, about 12 miles east by north of *Islamabad.* It may also be reached from several places in the *Liddar Valley,* as from *Harpat Nag, Liddroo,* and *Palgam,* also from the road between *Chandanwari* and *Sheesha Nag,* on the way to the *Cave of Ambernath;* these, however, are all footpaths across the mountains, and only fit for sportsmen and coolies.

The climate of the *Wardwan* is rigorous, and rain or snow falls throughout the greater part of the year ; it contains several thinly populated villages, whose inhabitants obtain a bare subsistence from the scanty products of their valley. Altogether, it is rather an inhospitable region, and interesting rather to the sportsman than to the general visitor, on account of its ibex grounds, for which it is greatly celebrated.

CHAPTER V.

WESTERN PORTION OF KASHMIR.

Table of rates by Doongah—Old gallows—Chowni—Grove of Sannybawan—Shadipore—Sind River—Noroo Canal—Gánderbal—Sumbal—Manasbal—Hajan—Banair—Woolar Lake—Lanka—Bandipore—Alsoo—Kewnas—Hill of Shukaroodeen—Sopoor—Pohra River—Awatkoola—Baramula—Gulmarg—Sonamarg—Lalab.

THE *objects of interest in the* Western portion of Kashmir are, the continuation of the *Jhelam*, which is navigable as far as *Baramula;* the *Sind* and *Pohra* Rivers, which enter its right bank and are both navigable for many miles when the water is high; the *Manasbal* and *Woolar Lakes*, *Gulmarg*, *Sonamarg*, and the *Lolab*. A part of this tour may be accomplished by water; the visitor may engage one or more *doongahs* for himself, his servants and baggage, and his horses can march along the banks of the rivers and lakes, orders being given where they are to meet the boats.

Time Table for journeys by Doongah to places on the Rivers and Lakes West of Srinagar.

Average time occupied.	From / To		To / From		Average time occupied.
6 hours	Srinagar	...	Shádipore	...	4 hrs.
7 „	„	...	Gánderbal	...	8 „
12 „	„	...	Pattan	...	8 „
12 „	„	...	Palhallan	...	8½ „
8 „	„	...	Súmbal	...	5½ „
10 „	„	...	Manasbal	...	7 „
12 „	„	...	Hajan	..	8 „
15 „	„	...	Lanka Island	...	10 „
16 „	„	...	Bandipoora	...	12 „
17 „	„	...	Alsoo	...	13 „
18 „	„	...	Kewnus	...	14 „
14 „	„	...	Sopoor	...	10 „
26 „	„	...	Awatkoola	...	30 „
20 „	„	...	Baramúla	...	13½ „

The DUDHGANGA RIVER is seen opening on the left, just after passing under the last bridge or *Saffa Kadal*. A little lower down, upon the same side, is the old GALLOWS, from which, in former times, one or more bodies might always be seen hanging. No execution has taken place here for many years; indeed, capital punishment is now rare in Kashmir, as the religious tenets of the Maharajah discourage the taking of human life : before an execution can be carried out, the warrant must be submitted to him upon three separate occasions and signed each time in the presence of the chief ministers of State.

The CHOWNI is on the left, about a mile below the last bridge, and consists of a fine grove of poplars, available for the encampment of visitors.

The GROVE OF SUNNYBAWAN—a clump of *chenars*—is about three miles below the *Chowni*, and upon the right, it is a pleasant place for encampment, and there is a village just behind it from whence a few supplies may be obtained.

SHADIPORE is a very small village on the left a few miles below this grove, and about four hours' journey by water from Srinagar; its name signifies *the place of marriage*, for here the *Sind* effects a junction with the *Jhelam*.

The SIND RIVER is about 100 yards wide at its mouth, and varies in depth from 3 to 18 feet; it is navigable from *Shádipore* to *Gánderbal* in the early part of the season, and the journey occupies about four or five hours; there are several villages along its banks, and some groves of trees suitable for encampment. The *Gánderbal* ghât is about a quarter of a mile above the mouth of a small stream about 36 feet wide, which joins the left bank of the river; across this stream is one of the arches of a ruined stone bridge, probably the longest in Kashmir, and which appears to have consisted of not less than twelve arches; its length was about 120 yards, and it formerly spanned the *Sind*, which now, however, flows several yards to the west of it. *Gánderbal* is a small village about a mile from the ghât, and beneath a lateral spur from the mountains which is composed of excellent *kankar* (nummular limestone), and upon which the *prungus* plant grows abundantly; the *Sind Valley* and *Sonamarg*, subsequently described, may be visited from it, and coolies and provisions are procurable.

In the bed of the *Jhelam* just below the junction of the *Sind*, is a mass of solid masonry, about 55 yards from the right bank of the river, 25 feet long, 16 feet wide, and 8 feet deep, and resting upon a broad and stony foundation about 12 feet above the bed of the river. It is a Hindú place of worship dedicated to *Mahadeo*, and its top is reached by seven stone steps, which are placed at its lower end. On the 15th August, 1865, the trunk of the chenar which, tradition says, never grows, was about 11 feet in circumference, and surrounded by an earthen platform one foot high and 6½ feet square, and pierced by several small branches of the tree; upon the western side of this platform there was a large *lingam*, whose base was ornamented with a garland of flowers, and a quantity of the red pigment with which the Hindús paint their foreheads and other parts of their bodies.

This place—like the precipice above the cataract of *Haribal*—is said to have been the scene of many an act of self-immolation; it was here, and in the presence of a vast multitude of people, that the faithful *dewan* of the great King *Lalitaditya* committed suicide by drowning himself, as related in the *Rajtaringini.*

The NOROO CANAL leaves the left bank of the river immediately below *Shadipore;* it is about 36 yards wide, and varies in depth according to the state of the river; there is a block of masonry in the middle of it, apparently the remains of a bridge. The canal runs southwards, and after a few miles divides into two branches, the smaller of which continues straight on towards *Pálhallan,* while the other turns to the right and finally enters the southern portion of the *Woolar Lake.* When the water is high enough, this, which is the shorter route, is always selected by the boatmen when passing between *Srinagar* and *Baramula,* so that they may avoid going through the Woolar, where, in the early part of the season, squalls are very frequent, and often as sudden and violent as they are dangerous.

The NARAIN BAGH is an old pleasure garden on the right bank of the *Sind,* close to its junction with the *Jhelam,* and its site is indicated by a fine grove of chenars. Just opposite the solitary chenar, and on the right bank of the river, there is a Hindu temple commenced by the late *Pundit Rájika* to the memory of *Golab Singh:* he was the minister of shawls, and to him was attributed the serious riot which occurred amongst the weavers in Srinagar on the 29th of April, 1865. He died shortly after this event, and—according to careful enquiries made by the author—most probably from a paralytic stroke.

The Surij Bagh, or Dab Bagh, is a ruined pleasure garden, about ten minutes' walk from a ghât on the right bank of the river, and about half a mile below *Shadipore.* It was made in 1820 by *Surij Bahri,* a collector of taxes under *Moti Ram,* the first Viceroy appointed to Kashmir after its conquest by *Ranjit Singh.* It was laid out somewhat in the manner of the *Nishat,* and when visited in 1835 by *Baron Hügel,* who describes it in his *Travels in Kashmir,* it was kept in good order; it is now neglected and in ruins, although there are still some good fruit-trees, grapes, and some very fine chenars in it.

Sumbal is a small village on the *Jhelam* and about an hour and a half's journey by boat below *Shadipore;* there is a bridge across the river, which is here about 112 yards broad, and on its left bank are two fine groves of chenars, one above, and the other below, the bridge—both situable for encampment.

MANASBAL is the most beautiful lake in Kashmir, and is connected with the *Jhelam* by a canal which opens into its right bank at *Naynároo*, a small village surrounded by some large mulberry-trees, about 400 yards below *Sumbal*, and 5½ hours' journey by boat from Srinagar. The canal is about 20 yards wide, and varies in depth according to the height of the river; it is about a mile long from its mouth to its junction with the lake, and the passage by boat occupies about twenty minutes; it is crossed about 100 yards from the river by an old stone bridge of one arch, 13 feet wide and very convex. The lake is oblong in shape, and its direction north-east and south-west; it is about three miles long and one mile wide, and the journey from one end to the other by *doongah* occupies about an hour. It is the deepest of all the lakes in Kashmir, being in some parts upwards of 40 feet; in Hindú legends it is represented as unfathomable, and it is related that one holy man spent several years in making a line long enough to reach the bottom of it, but at length, despairing of success, he threw himself into it, and never rose again. The water is clear, soft, of a deep-green colour, and chiefly derived from internal springs; when the water is low, many of these may be seen around its margins, and some of them are like miniature fountains, ejecting small columns of sand. Water-plants abound in its shallower parts, particularly the white and red lotuses, which begin to flower early in July; some of them are exceedingly fine, the leaves being 24 inches in diameter, and some of the petioles 12 feet long. The view from the entrance of the lake is very pretty; on the left is an elevated table-land composed chiefly of *kankar*, and below it and near the edge of the water is the small village of *Mánasbal;* above and beyond are the ruins of the *Badshah Bagh*, consisting of an old palace and garden built by *Jehangir* for his wife, the lovely *Nurmahal;* and beyond these again is the small village from whence the supplies for visitors are mostly obtained. On the right is a low range of hills extending from the lofty mountains on the north-east; the conical peak is called the *Aha Thang;* it is 6,290 feet high, and visible from many distant parts of the valley. Beyond it, at the foot of the range, and upon the margin of the lake, is the large village of *Kundbal*, which contains a great many lime-kilns, from whence the city of Srinagar is chiefly supplied; the limestone is procured from the adjoining hills, and the wood for burning it is conveyed from the forests of the *Sind Valley.* In front is a range of very high mountains, mostly bare and rugged; at the foot of them, and beyond *Kundbal,* is a fine cataract formed by the *Amrawattee* stream falling over the white and steep limestone cliff into the lake below. A few feet from this fall, and standing in the water, is a small Hindú ruin, whose four sides are each about 6½ feet wide; it has a pyramidal roof about 12 feet above the bed of the lake, and there is an opening on the southern side with the usual trefoil archway.

There is no bungalow at *Manasbal*, and visitors usually encamp at the foot of the mountains, at the further end of the lake, where there is a fine grove of chenars, and some other pleasant spots; there is a stream behind the grove, conveyed from the *Sind River:* the water is very cold, and forms an excellent substitute for ice for cooling purposes. There is also a fakir's orchard close by, the peaches of which are unsurpassed in any other part of the valley. The fakir is digging his grave in the orchard, in the form of a cave, which in 1865, was about 50 feet long. The climate of *Manasbal* is very salubrious, and it is a very favorite and convenient retreat from Srinagar, especially during the unhealthy months of July and August. The hills around the lake command extensive views of the central portion of the valley; the mouth of the *Sind Valley* is only two or three miles distant, and is visible towards the north-east: the city of *Srinagar* and its environs are also visible on the east; the *Woolar Lake* lies to the west, and is overlooked by the hoary *Haramuk,* near which may be seen a gap, through which lies the road to *Gurais* and *Iskardó;* the winding *Jhelam* may be seen towards the south, also the mountains which enclose *Gulmarg,* to the right of which is a deep gap, in which lies the *Báramúla Pass. Sonamarg* is only four marches distant.

HAJAN is a large village on the left bank of the *Jhelam,* about 2½ hours' journey by boat below *Súmbal.*

Just below it is one of the numerous *Royal Studs,* which is well worth visiting; large droves of ponies will have been noticed in various places along the river side. Adjoining this stud, and overshadowed by some very fine *Chenars* is a small *zearat* of the great Saint *Shukarúdín,* whose tomb at *Chrar,* near Rámoo, is perhaps the most frequented of the Mahomedan shrines in Kashmir.

BANAIR is the name given to the marshy plain lying between the two branches of the *Jhelam,* which are formed just before it enters the *Woolar Lake;* excellent mahseer and other fishing may be found here, especially on the left bank of the right or larger branch of the river.

The WOOLAR LAKE is the largest in Kashmir; it is about ten hours' journey by boat from *Srinagar,* and the *Jhelam* flows through it. It is a magnificent piece of water, irregularly oval in shape; its greatest width from east to west is about 10 miles, and its length from north to south about 12 miles; its average depth is 12 feet, the deepest part being on its western side, opposite the hill of *Shúkarudín*, where it is about 16 feet. The water is clear, and derived partly from internal springs and partly from mountain streams, of which the *Erin* and *Bandipoor* nallahs on the north-east are the chief. Its bed is composed of soft mud, and where it is shallow its surface is covered with water-plants. It is enclosed on the east and north by very lofty mountains whose sides are comparatively bare of trees, and slope gently down to its margin; the space between the foot of the mountains and the edge of the lake varies from a few hundred yards to a mile or more according to the the height of the water; but it is always greater on the northern than on the eastern side. There is a good bridle road all round its northern half, from *Manasbal* and *Arjas* on the east, to *Watlab* and *Sopoor* on the west. Its shores are studded with numerous villages, which are mostly occupied by persons engaged in collecting its various products, the chief of which are the *singhara* or water-nut, *fish* and *lotuses*, which all yield a large revenue; during the cold weather it also swarms with water-fowl. A day or two may well be occupied in visiting the various objects of interest about it, and the following are the principal of them :—

The Lanka.—This is an island on the right, just at the entrance of the lake, and is said to have been raised by the Mahomedan King *Zinal-abú-dín;* there are some very old ruins upon it, and it is the subject of numerous traditions. The surface of the water around it is covered to the extent of a mile or so, by the *lotus* and *singhara* plants, which are so thick that when the water is low it cannot be approached by a *doongah,* but only by a *shikárah;* and in July and August the mosquitoes are innumerable and excessively troublesome. It it quadrangular in shape, and its longer sides, which are north and south, are about 95 yards long, and its shorter, which are east and west, about 75 yards; it is densely covered with trees, chiefly mulberry, and they are entwined by grape vines of the *sahibi* or red variety, which yield excellent fruit in the month of August. There is a ruined *stone building* near its eastern corner, which in shape resembles that at *Martand,* but differs from it in being much smaller, and in having two tiers of trefoil arches instead of one; it is roofless, consists of two apartments, the larger of which measures, internally 30 by 26 feet, and its massive walls are all tottering; that upon the north side seems to have fallen recently, and to have been caused chiefly by the growing roots of the mulberry trees. There is also a small *brick building* near the north-western corner, the outside of which was formerly entirely covered with blue enamelled slabs, of which some are still remaining; it consists of one room 16 feet square, with a dome-shaped roof—an entrance on the northern and another on the eastern side; there is an old Mahomedan cemetery on its southern side; and in a recess inside the building there is a detached stone slab with a Persian inscription upon it, from which it appears that the *Lanka* was constructed by *Shah Zainibad* or *Zinal-abu-din* about A.D. 1411. Numerous large and rectangular masses of carved stones are seen around the margins of the island, apparently the remains of an ornamental stone wall. Along its southern side are several fragments of sculptured stones and broken pillars, also a flight of stone steps, on one side of which is a stone trough, and on the other a large *lingam* standing in the water. On its easteru side there are numerous carved masses and pillars, and the half of one is standing erect near the stone building. On its northern side are many carved masses, but only one pillar, and lying near a flight of stone steps, which are almost entirely worn away. On its western side are also a few masses, but no pillars. The carved masses are all large and mostly quadrilateral in shape, and the pillars are all fluted limestone columns about 8½ feet high and 4 feet 4 inches in circumference; those lying upon the eastern and southern sides are in a fair state of preservation, but those upon the northern side are considerably worn, while those on the western side are so much so, that the carving is scarcely traceable. The difference in the condition of these ruined fragments, according to their situation, is very striking, and suggests a question of great interest as to the cause.

BANDIPOOR is a considerable town on the north-eastern side of the Woolar, and about a mile and a half from its margin; when the water is high, it may be approached within a few hundred yards by a nullah, which flows near it and empties itself into the lake; the journey by boat from the *Lunka* to the mouth of this nallah occupies about an hour. The town contains nothing of special interest; there is a shady encamping ground in front of it, but no visitors' bungalow; it is the starting point for the *Goorais* district, and for *Gilgit* and *Iskardo*, the route to which will be found at No. 18, in Montgomerie's *Kashmir Route Map.* The *Gungabal*, a lake on the top of the *Haramuk*, lies to the east, and may be reached in two stages by marching across the mountains. The distance by land from *Bandipoor* to *Sopoor* is about 16 miles; the road is mostly smooth and level, and leads round the northern shores of the Woolar. *Naopore* is a small village a few minutes' walk to the west of *Bandipoor;* and *Kewlus*—which contains a thannah—is about a mile further on. After passing *Kanjipore* on the right, and *Watpora* on the left, the road leads to the village of *Potshai*, about five miles from *Bandipoor*, and about a mile beyond it is the small village of *Manganpora*.

ALSOO or ALOOS is situated on the slope of the hill about a mile from the shore; there is a road passing over the hills from it to *Lálpoor*, the chief town in the *Lolab*, and about five koss distant towards the west-north-west. *Kewnus* is a village about three miles beyond *Alsoo*, and about four hours' journey by boat from *Bandipoor;* it is situated in a nook about a quarter of a mile from the edge of the lake, and is surrounded by fruit-trees and grape vines. *Lálpoor* may also be reached from it by a path leading over the hills, and it is about five koss distant.

The HILL OF SHUKARUDIN is the higher of the two eminences at the end of the spur which runs down from the mountains on the western side of the lake; it is about 700 feet high, and may be ascended on horseback either from the *Kewnus* side, or from *Watlab*, a small village upon its southern side. The ascent from *Kewnus* occupies about half an hour; it commences about half a mile from the village, and at a small spring which is almost concealed by a clump of trees. The path is rather steep and rough; there are large blocks of stone in some parts, of a greenish colour, and which contain masses of pure white quartz. The *zearat* of *Baba Shu-*

karudin—a venerable Rishi, and one of the disciples of the great *Shah Núrúdin*—occupies the summit of the hill; it is an old and dilapidated building of the usual kind, but commands a splendid view of the western portion of the valley. The Woolar is seen below in all its beauty, and with its shores studded by numerous villages; towards the east is the *Lanka*, and beyond it, lying under the *Aha Thang*, are the glittering waters of *Mánasbal;* towards the south, *Sopoor* and *Baramúla* are plainly seen, and also the high range of hills which overlook the beautiful downs of *Gulmarg*. The *Jhelam* may be seen entering the eastern side of the lake; after passing through it, it leaves it a short distance above *Sopoor*, thence winding to the westward it flows past *Baramúla*, and shortly escapes from the valley. There is a road from *Watlab* to *Sopoor*, which is about five miles distant by land; but the journey by boat occupies about four hours.

SOPOOR or *Surapur*—mentioned in the *Rajtaringini* in the 5th century—rebuilt by *Sura*, the minister of *Avante Verma* between A.D. 854 and 883—and the old name of which was *Kambura*—is a large but dilapidated town, built upon both sides of the *Jhelam*, and from ten to twelve hours' journey by boat below Srinagar: the two portions of the town are united by a bridge, half of which is of stone and the other half of wood. There is no pleasant encamping ground nor any large trees near it; but there are two commodious buildings for visitors, above the bridge, and on the right bank of the river. There is a stone fort on the right, just above the bridge, quadrangular in shape, of some strength, and now used as a thánnah: below it, and on the right, is a Hindú temple with a large *lingam* outside it; and nearly opposite, on the other side of the river, is a pretty mosque with gilded spires, near which is the Government Dispensary. *Sopoor* is considered the best place in the valley for mahseer fishing; *Gulmarg* and the *Lólab* may both be visited from it, and the routes are described in subsequent sections.

The POHRA RIVER joins the right bank of the *Jhelam* at the village of *Dabgao*, which is about an hour and a half's journey by boat below *Sopoor*, and consists of a few houses surrounded by a fine grove of *chenars*, occupied by the agents attached to the adjoining Goverment timber depôt. The *Pohra* is about 75 yards wide at its mouth, but varies in depth according to the season; it rises in the mountains on the north-west of the valley, and receives in its course numerous tributaries from the adjacent hills. In the early part of the season it is a fine river, and navigable for *doongahs* as far as *Awatkoola*, a small and half-deserted village on its left bank, about twenty hours' journey by boat from *Dabgao*, and the chief starting point for the *Lólab*.

BARAMULA is a large town on the right bank of the *Jhelam*, at the western end of the valley, about 3½ hours' journey by boat from *Sopoor* and about fourteen hours' journey by boat from *Srinagar*, by the *Noroo Canal* route; it is situated at the foot of a lofty range of hills, and contains about 250 houses, many of which are very old and ruinous. The boats can, but do not usually, go beyond the town, but the river, which is here about 150 yards wide, may be seen winding for some distance between the lofty mountains; after three or four miles it leaves the valley, and shortly becomes a rough and roaring torrent. There are two bungalows for visitors, both upon the left bank, and about 150 yards above the bridge, and near a fine large orchard, which is a pleasant place for encampment; there is an old fort at the left end of the bridge, and the ruins of an old Mogul *serai* at its right; close by on the left there is a shrine worthy of a visit. The *Marri* road passes over the hills to the south-west, and the *Abbottabad* road along the right bank of the river. *Gulmarg* may be reached from it by two roads, a pony-road and a footpath; they both lead towards the south, and are described in the following section. At *Ushkarah*, about a mile to the south-east, are the ruins of a temple.

GULMARG.

GULMARG—the favorite sanitarium for July and August—is one of those mountain downs, or grassy valleys, which are numerous upon the top of the hills immediately below the *Pir Panjál,* and upon the slopes of the mountains enclosing the northern side of the valley. These *margs*—most of which are marked in the *Jamoo and Kashmir Map*—are covered with rich pasturage, and during the summer large herds of ponies, cattle, sheep, and goats are sent up from the plains to graze, and they remain there in charge of the *gulubans* or horse-keepers, *gujarus* or cowherds, and *chopans* or *pahals* or shepherds, until the beginning of the cold weather, when they return to winter in the valley. *Gulmarg* lies to the westward of *Srinagar,* from whence it may be reached by several routes, of which the following are the principal, viz :—

1. BY LAND ALL THE WAY VIA KHANDAHAMA.
2. BY LAND ALL THE WAY VIA PATTAN.
3. BY BOAT TO PALHALLAN AND THENCE BY LAND.
4. BY BOAT TO SOPOOR AND THENCE BY LAND.
5. BY BOAT TO BARAMULA AND THENCE BY LAND.

1. BY LAND ALL THE WAY VIA KHANDAHAMA.—This is the shortest route, and may be accomplished in two stages; first, from *Srinagar* to *Khandahama,* about 14 miles; second, from *Khandahama viâ Ferozepore* to

Gulmarg about 9 miles. The first stage is easy, but second is very rough: the *Suknág* and several other streams have to be forded; and although practicable for riding ponies, the baggage had better be sent by coolies.

2. BY LAND ALL THE WAY VIA PATTAN.—This is a good pony-road, and is reckoned two stages and a half; the *first stage* is from *Srinagar* to *Pattan,* and is about 17 miles; the road is level, and passes over the *Ameeri Kadal,* down the avenue of poplars near the entrance to the *Sher Garhi,* then turns to the right leading through the suburbs of *Chatterbal,* and thence through the fields to *Pattan.* On the right side of the road, and within about half a mile of *Pattan,* there are two large ruined temples close to each other, in a good state of preservation, and well worthy of a special visit. *Pattan* is now an old and ruinous village, but was once a place of some importance; it is situated on the high road to *Baramúla,* under the northern edge of a large *kareewah,* and surrounded by some very fine *chenars.*

The *second stage* is from *Pattan* to *Babamirishi,* and is 12½ miles; the road turns to the south-west, soon ascends the *kareewah* behind the village and passes up to *Chandesir,* a small village about five miles from *Pattan,* and where the road from *Palhallan* joins that from *Pattan.* *Khipore* is a large village about three miles further on; a fine stream of cold water passes through it, near which are some shady trees very pleasant for half-way breakfast. An easy ascent through fields and forest then leads to *Ajeebal*, about three miles further on. *Babamirishi*—about 1½ miles beyond it, and reached by a tolerably smooth but rather steep ascent through park-like scenery—is a small and sloping grassy plain on the top of the lower range of hills, and derives its name from the adjoining *zearat* of *Baba Pyoomdeen*, a Rishi, who died about 400 years ago; he is deeply venerated by the Mahomedans, and his shrine—to which is attached a monastery—is one of the richest as well as one of the most frequented places of pilgrimage in Kashmir. There is a wooden pavilion upon the green and sloping plateau above, and to the left of the *zearat* built by the priests in 1864 for the use of visitors; it consists of a raised room 16 feet long, and about 12 feet wide, surrounded by lattice-work, and from which there is a very extensive view of the valley. *Babamirishi* is cool and very healthy, and is a favorite encamping place during the months of July and August, the fall of rain being less than at *Gulmarg*, which is more than 1,000 feet above it.

The *remaining half stage* is from *Babamirishi* to the usual encamping ground at *Gulmarg*; it is about 1½ miles by the pony-road, and the journey occupies about an hour. The first half mile is steep, but tolerably wide and smooth, and opens into a narrow defile, where the road is green and level; at the end of another half mile it opens into the main valley and turning to the left leads to the encamping ground, about half a mile distant, and at the extremity of a long and wooded spur on the right. A foot-path leaves the pony-road a few hundred yards beyond *Babamirishi*, and passing up to the left opens into *Gulmarg,* nearly opposite the encamping ground; it is short, but steep and narrow, and only fit for coolies.

3. BY BOAT TO PALHALLAN, AND THENCE BY LAND.—*Pálhallan* is situated near the southern margin of an extensive morass, and can only be reached by water when the river is high. The boats pass down the *Jhelam* to *Shadipore* in about four hours, then along the *Noroo Canal*, and cross the morass to *Pálhallan,* which is near the western side of the morass, and about 4½ hours' journey from *Shadipore.* This morass is several miles in extent, shallow, densely covered with rushes and other water-plants, and during the later months it swarms with mosquitoes, which render the passage across it exceedingly disagreeable. PALHALLAN is an extensive village surrounded by grassy slopes, shaded by magnificent *chenars*, and about a mile and a half from the ghât; there is no bangalow, but coolies and tattoos are usually procurable at a

short notice; the rate for the former is one anna each, and for the latter two annas from the ghât to the village. The distance from *Pálhallan* to *Gulmarg* is about twelve miles, and is reckoned a stage and a half; the road leads to the south, and joins the *Pattan* road to *Babamirishi*, just beyond *Chandesir*, and about three miles from *Pálhallan;* the coolies get over the whole journey in about six hours.

4. BY BOAT TO SOPOOR AND THENCE BY LAND.—This is the easiest, most convenient, and prettiest of all the routes. *Sopoor* is situated on the *Jhelam*, and about ten or twelve hours' journey by boat from *Srinagar;* the boats pass down the river to *Shadipore*, and when the water is high enough, along the *Noroo Canal*, the safer and shorter way; but when it is low, they continue down the river, and through the *Woolar Lake.* There is a good pony-road all the way from *Sopoor* to *Gulmarg;* the distance is about 17½ miles, and is reckoned two stages. The *first stage* is from *Sopoor* to *Kountra*, distance 12½ miles, and the road wide and easy all the way; after skirting the edge of the *Woolar*, it passes by *Lálad*, a village on the right, at the mouth of a wide valley between two *kareewahs*, and about two miles from *Sopoor;* thence it passes to *Naopore*, a ruined village about two miles further on, and where, on the right, it is joined by the

pony-road from *Baramúla*. A few hundred yards further on, the road ascends the *kareewah* on the left, and crossing it, opens into the valley of the *Ningil River*, which is crossed by a wooden bridge just beyond the village of *Shackwara;* thence it continues along the right bank of the river, gradually ascending and passing through the villages of *Wogoor* and *Mainagam* up to *Kountra*, a considerable village prettily situated on the hill side, and overlooking the *Ningil* valley, here about half a mile wide; there is no bungalow, but there are some pleasant spots for encampment; the foot-path from *Baramúla* joins the road here.

The *second stage* is from *Kountra* to *Gulmarg*, distance about five miles; the road turns to the left, and passing through a gap, shortly enters a green and narrow glen, traversed by a small stream, which has to be forded about nine times. This pretty glen is called *Nambalnár*, and contains two or three small villages belonging to the *zearat* of *Babamirishi;* after a very easy rise of about two miles, the path leads to the foot of the mountains, from whence there is a steep and rather rough ascent of about half a mile through lovely scenery to *Babamirishi*, described in a previous page, where will also be found the continuation of this route to *Gulmarg*.

5. BY BOAT TO BARAMULA AND THENCE BY LAND. —BARAMULA is a large town situated on the right bank

of the *Jhelam*, at the western end of the valley, and about fourteen hours' journey by boat (*via* the *Noroo Canal*) from *Srinagar*. There are two roads from *Baramúla* to *Gulmarg*—a *pony-road*, which joins the road from *Sopoor* just beyond the village of *Naopore*, and a *foot-path*, which joins the same road at *Kountra*. The distance by the pony-road is about 16 miles, by the foot-path about 14 miles; the journey by each may be accomplished in one march, and occupies about six hours, but carriage must be paid for at the rate of a stage and a half.

GULMARG is a beautiful mountain common nearly 3,000 feet above the level of *Srinagar*, about three miles long, and varies in width from a few hundred yards to more than a mile; its direction is chiefly north-west and south-east, and it is bounded on all sides by hills, from which numerous spurs, in the form of grassy knolls, project far into it. The whole surface of the *marg* and the projecting knolls are clothed with flowers of every hue, and hence its name,—from *gul* a flower, and *marg* a mountain-meadow; the surrounding hills are densely covered with forests; it is intersected by a stream which enters its south-eastern extremity, and receives numerous tributaries in its course towards the north-west, where it escapes through a deep gorge. At the north-eastern corner is the pony-road leading down to *Babamirishi;* at the south-eastern end is the rather steep and very rough pony-road leading down to the village of *Ferozpore,* and in the middle of the north-eastern side is the foot-path leading to *Babamirishi.* The climate of *Gulmarg* is cool, bracing, and salubrious, and although the rainfall is very considerable, it is a justly favorite sanitarium for visitors, especially during the months of July and August. There are several log huts, but visitors usually encamp upon the top of one of the numerous knolls, where wood for the log-fire, so enjoyable at night, is abundant. Milk and butter may be procured in any quantity from the *gujurus* or cowherds about the *marg,* but other supplies must be obtained from the villages below, except when the Officers on duty are encamped there.

KILLAN is another *marg* about 1,000 feet above *Gulmarg,* than which it is longer and wider, and although it contains numerous springs, it is not nearly so pretty, and the rainfall is much greater. It is about three miles from *Gulmarg,* and may be reached by several foot-paths, and a pony-road, which lead through the dense and magnificent pine forest upon its south-western side; it is bounded by the snowy *Pir Panjal,* whose deeper gullies and ravines contain perpetual snow, which stretches across them like a roof and overlies the streams which flow beneath; one of these glaciers at the south-eastern corner of the *marg* is well worth visiting.

RAMPORE, one march from *Baramúla* on the *Marri Road*, may be reached by a path from *Gulmarg* in two stages; it is hardly practicable for dandies, except in very dry weather; the distance is about 18 miles, and the whole journey occupies about 10 hours. The path leaves the *marg* through the gorge on the north-west, and is tolerably smooth and level as far as the village of *Chorkuda*, 9 miles distant; at first it leads through a thick forest, then over a succession of six *margs* across a couple of mountain streams, one of which is bridged and the other has to be forded; the villages of *Nagree*, *Nao*, and *Saonlee Allee* are passed on the way; the latter is about 8 miles from *Gulmarg*, and is a convenient place for breakfast. Just opposite *Nao*, and on the right, is a foot-path leading over the mountains to *Baramúla*, said to be 5 *koss* distant; and 200 or 300 yards beyond *Saonlee Allee*, there is a foot-path leading down a ravine on the left towards *Ooree*, said to be 8 *koss* distant. The portion of the road from *Chorkúda* to *Naoshera* is a steady descent, and leads nearly all the way through a dense forest, covering the side of a deep valley; the first two miles are steep but smooth, the next mile is smooth and tolerably level, but the remaining two miles are very steep, and in several places rough and rocky; the scenery, however, throughout is very fine indeed. *Rampore* is about 4 miles distant from *Naoshera*, and is described in the *Rawal Pindi and Marri Route.*

SOORAN, on the *Bhimber* and *Púnch Road*, may also be reached by a path from *Gulmarg;* it is practicable for dandies, and the distance is divided into four stages as follows:—

Route from Gulmarg to Sooran on the Bhimber and Púnch Road.

No.	Names.	Distance.	REMARKS.
	From Gulmarg	Miles.	
1	To Barzatah	12	No village: an encamping ground.
2	Gagri	15	A small village.
3	Mandi	10	A large town.
4	Sooran	15	A small village.

1. From *Gulmarg* to *Barzatah*, 12 miles. The road passes up behind *Gulmarg*, through the forest, across the *Killan* marg, over the range behind it, and into a valley on the other side; it is rather steep, but tolerably smooth. *Barzatah* is simply an encamping ground in the mountains, and except milk and butter from the cowherds, neither supplies nor coolies are obtainable.

2. From *Barzatah* to *Gagri*, 15 miles. The *Pir Panjal* has to be crossed by the *Ferozepore Pass* in this stage; the ascent is easy, but the descent is very steep and occasionally rough; in some places the road passes

over small nullahs bridged by hardened snow, and at the bottom of the descent a large stream has to be forded. *Gagri* is a small village, but a few supplies and coolies are procurable.

3. From *Gagri* to *Mandi*, 10 miles. This is an easy stage; the road passes mostly along the banks of the stream, with a few gentle ups and downs. *Mandi* is a large village, containing the summer residence of *Moti Singh*, the Rajah of Púnch; supplies of food and coolies are usually abundant.

4. From *Mandi* to *Sooran*, 15 miles. This is also an easy stage; towards the latter half of it the path joins the Púnch road, at the junction of the above stream with the *Sooran River*, and then turning to the left, it continues up the valley to *Sooran*, which is described in Chapter II. in the section on the *Bhimber and Púnch Route.*

The Sind Valley, Wangat Ruins, and Sonamarg.

The Sind Valley is in the *Lár* pergunnah, and lies a few miles north of Srinagar; it is long and very narrow, its direction is mostly east and west, and it is bounded on both sides by very high mountains; it extends from near *Gánderbal* on the west to the *Zojila Pass* on the east, a distance of about 58 miles; and its breadth varies from a few hundred yards to about half a mile. It owes its name to the *River Sind,* which rises in the mountains near the *Cave of Ambernáth*, and enters the head of the valley through a deep and rocky defile beyond *Sonamarg;* the water is of a deep-green color, derived chiefly from the melting snows, and is very cold; in its course it receives numerous tributaries from the adjoining mountains; its bed is very rocky; it is noisy and rapid, floating large quantities of timber down from the adjacent forests to *Mánasbal* and *Gánderbal;* and it joins the *Jhelam* at *Shadipore.*

The scenery of the valley is very grand and beautiful; on either side are lofty mountains, whose tops are usually crowned with snow, whose sides, more or less precipitous, are clothed with large forests of pine, and whose feet are lined with walnut, chesnut, sycamore, and many other kinds of trees. Several smaller valleys open into it, which are also traversed by streams running down to mingle with the waters of the Sind: one of these near *Kangan* gives passage to the *Kanknai River.* Numerous small villages, surrounded by patches of cultivation, lie scattered along the banks of the river; and the ground, carpetted with rich grass, is shaded by wild fruit-trees, as peaches, apricots, apples, pears, grapes, and plums. The climate of the valley is considered the healthiest in Kashmir; it is a favorite resort for the upper classes of natives during the malarious months of July and August, and its fruits, especially the grapes, are regarded as the choicest in the Valley. Large game abounds, particularly in the higher ranges on its northern side, and towards the *Tilail* valley, which are amongst the finest hunting grounds around Kashmir. The *Ladak Road*—the great highway between Kashmir and Central Asia—passes through it, usually close to the river, and mostly along its right bank; it is practicable for ponies and mules, and the route from *Srinagar* to *Leh*, the capital of *Ladák*, is as follows:—

Route from Srinagar to Leh by the Drás Road.

1	Srinagar to Ganderbal ...	14	
2	Kangan	11	
3	Gond	14	
4	Gagangair	9	
5	Sonamarg	10	
6	Baltal	9	
7	Mataiyun	15	Cross the Zojila Pass.
8	Drás	15	
9	Tashgam	15	
10	Chenagoond	15	
11	Kargil	8	
12	Lochan...	13	
13	Moolbekh	11	
14	Charak	11	
15	Lama Yuru	19	
16	Kullach or Kulsi	12	
17	Hemis	15	
18	Basgo	17	
19	Leh	21	

The chief places of interest up the Sind Valley are the Ruins above Wangat, and Sonamarg; the former are those of *Rájdainbal* and *Nágbal;* they are amongst the oldest in Kashmir, and are situated at the upper end of a minor valley opening into that of the Sind, and above the village of *Wángat* about nine miles from *Gánderbal;* they may be visited in two marches from *Srinagar* according to the following route :—

	Route from Srinagar to ruins beyond Wangat.	Miles.	TOTAL.
No. 1.	From Srinagar		
	To Ameeri Kadal Fort	3	
	Noashera	3	
	Soroo	2	
	Malshabagh	4	
	Ganderbal	2	
			14 miles.

	Route from Srinagar to ruins beyond Wangat.	Miles.	TOTAL.
No. 2	From Ganderbal		
	To Noonar	3	
	Gutlibagh	3	
	Bridge...	1½	
	Drógdun	1½	
	Kachnambal	3	
	Wangat	3½	
	Ruins	2½	
			18 miles.

FROM SRINAGAR TO GANDERBAL.—*Distance* 14 *miles.*

The road is smooth, wide, and tolerably level all the way; it lies along the northern side of the city, passes near the fort and through *Naoshera*—a large village containing the Government paper manufactories. Between the fort and *Naoshera* are several ruins which deserve a special visit from the antiquarian; the principal one is that of a large stone temple, in the parish of *Zojibal* or *Zoribal*, standing upon the opposite edge of an extensive morass, a short distance from the road. About two miles beyond *Soroo* the road descends over a bed of *kankar* to the level of the *Anchar Lake*, which may be seen stretching far away to the left; a little beyond this a considerable stream passes underground by a subterranean channel, and re-appears some yards to the left; several springs may also be seen issuing in different places from the base of the hills upon the right. The most interesting objects, however, along this road are the enormous masses of shingle on the hill side just below *Malshabagh;* they are the remains of a beach more extensive than those at the mouth of the *Liddar Valley*, and are the strongest geological proof that, previous to the exit of the *Jhelam* through the gorge below *Baramúla*, the Valley of Kashmir was the bed of a magnificent mountain lake. *Gánderbal* may also be reached by water in the early part of the season, by passing down the *Jhelam* to *Shadipore,* and thence up the *River Sind* to the ghât, which is about a mile from the village, and which has been previously described.

FROM GANDERBAL TO THE RUINS.—*Distance* 18 *miles.*

There is a fair bridle-road all the way; it passes through cornfields to *Noonar*, a large village on the left, shortly afterwards enters the jungle and leads up to *Gutlibagh*, the first village within the *Sind Valley*. Just beyond this, a rather steep and rough descent occurs, and after about a quarter of a mile, another but shorter one leads down to the river, which is here about 25 yards wide and crossed by a rude and shaky wooden bridge. Thence it continues along the right bank of the river for about half a mile, passing over some rough places, and crossing the bridge over the stream which flows down from *Chittingool*, a village on the left, at the foot of the mountains. Leaving the *Ladak* Road, the path turns off to the left towards *Drógdun*, thence ascends through the fields to *Kachnambal*, whence it continues up the valley and along the right bank of the river all the way. This valley is an offshoot from that of the Sind; it is about six or eight miles long, not more than 500 yards wide, enclosed by very high and granitic mountains, and bounded at its upper extremity—where there is a road leading to the *Tilail* district—by a conical snowy mountain, on each side of which is a narrow defile traversed by a stream; by the union of these the river is formed which passes down the valley to join the *Sind*. *Wangat* is a small village near the upper end of the valley, and the last on the road; a few supplies may be obtained, and it is better to encamp here, as the ruins are only about two miles beyond.

RAJDAINBUL—the nearest of them—is the ruin of a magnificent stone temple, resembling those at *Martand* and *Awantipore;* it is situated near the upper end of the valley, about 100 yards from the right bank of the river, and consisted of four buildings enclosed by a stone wall, of which some portions are still standing. It is of great antiquity, and trees are growing through the roofs of the buildings. The ground within the enclosure is soft and marshy, as though it had formerly been the bed of a small lake, and the scenery around is as wild as can be imagined. NAGBAL is another ruin, about 150 yards beyond the above, and which it much resembles; there is a holy spring close to it—whence its name—issuing from the foot of the high mountains on the right side of the valley; the water is very cold and pure, and flows into a stone reservoir about 60 feet long and 40 feet wide. The ground, for some distance round, is thickly strewn with grass shoes, discarded by the pilgrims who visit the spring on their way to the Holy Lake *Gungabal,* which is situated upon the top of the *Haramuk,* the peak overlooking the valley; the ascent to it is steep and very fatiguing, and the journey up and down will occupy a whole day. The lake—according to Vigne—is about

1½ miles long and 250 yards wide; it is one of the mountain sources of the Jhelam, and is to the Hindus of Kashmir what the Ganges is to those of the plains of India. A great festival is held there annually, about the 20th August, and is attended by thousands of pilgrims from all the adjacent country.

SONAMARG, or the GOLDEN MEADOW, is a mountain down like *Gulmarg*, and almost equally popular as a sanitarium during the months of July and August, indeed, by many it is much preferred; a Christian Church was built there last year as well as a number of log houses for visitors. It is situated at the upper end of the *Sind Valley*, five marches from *Srinagar*, and the stages are given in the Route to *Leh*, on the high road to which it lies. The villages along the route are few and small, and provisions scarce; they had better, therefore, be taken from Srinagar, except when the Civil Officer on duty is encamped there, at which time they will be found abundant. The road is quite practicable for riding, and, as previously mentioned, the scenery and climate are most delightful—perhaps the best throughout Kashmir; were it not for its greater distance from *Srinagar*, it would be much more popular than *Gulmarg*.

THE LOLAB.

LOLAB is one of the prettiest pregunnahs in Kashmir; it lies on the north-western side of the province, and in that division of it called *Kamráj*; it consists of a beautiful undulating and fertile valley, oval in shape, about 15 miles in length, varying in width from a few hundred yards to three miles, surrounded by low hills clothed by dense pine forests, and traversed by a considerable stream. It contains about 30 villages, of which *Lálpoor* is the chief, and they are mostly situated in the midst of groves of walnuts and chenárs. It is a favorite place for visitors, who have ten or twelve days to spare to march about from village to village; indeed its charming scenery, its cool and invigorating climate, the ease of marching, and the usual abundance of supplies, render it one of the most attractive portions of Kashmir. Bears are very common there in the fruit-season, and they abound to such an extent in the forest on its northern side, that it may there be realy called a "Bear Garden."

Lálpoor, the chief town, may be reached be several routes, of which the following are the principal:—

1. From Alsoo or Kewnas.
2. From Sopoor via Arwan.
3. From Awatkoola.

1. From Alsoo or Kewnas.—These are two villages on the north-western shores of the *Woolar Lake*: *Lálpoor* is about ten miles from each of them, and is reached by a foot-path which crosses over the range of hills behind them.

2. From Sopoor via Arwan.—The distance from *Sopoor* to *Lálpoor* is about sixteen or seventeen miles, and is reckoned two stages: *first* from *Sopoor to Arwan,* a small village about nine miles north of *Sopoor*, situated at the foot of the hills, and containing some iron-works; the road is smooth, level, and very pretty. *Second*, from *Arwan* to *Lálpoor* the distance is about eight miles; the path leads over a range of hills about 8,000 feet high; the ascent is occasionally rather steep and rough, but the descent is easier; the scenery is very fine, and the summit of the range commands a very extensive view of the valley; *Lálpoor* is about four miles from the foot of the range.

3. From Awatkoola.—*Awatkoola* is a small and half-deserted village on the left bank of the *Pohra River*, about twenty hours' journey by boat from the village of *Dabgao*, at which the *Pohra* joins the *Jhelam*, and which is about an hour and a half's journey by boat below *Sopoor*. This is the easiest and most agreeable route, but can only be adopted when the river is high; about half-way up from *Dabgao* the *Pohra* becomes narrowed by rocks; its bed is here very rough, and the stream so strong that it is usually necessary to obtain assistance from the adjoining village to pull the boats through the rapids. There are several villages and groves of trees along its banks, and the scenery, especially in the latter

half of the journey, is very pretty. *Chogul* is a large village where a few supplies may generally be obtained; it is on the right bank, and about three miles beyond the rapids. About four or five miles below *Awatkoola* the river turns to the right, and after passing through a gap in the low range of hills, it becomes narrow, deep, slow, and smooth. and its banks, now high and sloping, are covered with various kinds of trees and shrubs having quite an English aspect.

There are two roads from *Awatkoola* to *Lálpoor*—a *foot-path* which leads over the range of hills to the north-east, and a *pony-road* which passes round the foot of the range towards the north-west, and near *Kofwára* it leads through a narrow glen covered with forest and traversed by the *Lolâb River*. The foot-path is only about 12 miles long, but both the ascent and descent are steep, rather rough, and only fit for coolies and led horses; the pony-road is about 18 miles long, and is level and tolerably smooth all the way; the scenery along them both is exceedingly fine.

From *Lálpoor*, which is a very small town, but prettily situated, the visitor may select his return route either by *Warpoora* to *Sopoor*, or he may visit the dense forests on the south-west, and thence proceed to *Báramúla* in order to quit the Vale of Kashmir, the tour of which is now completed.

THE END.

APPENDIX.

APPENDIX No. 1.

Treaty of Amritsar.

TREATY between the British Government on the one part, and Maharajah Golab Singh of Jummo on the other, concluded, on the part of the British Government, by Frederick Currie, Esq., and Brevet-Major Henry Montgomery Lawrence, acting under the orders of the Right Hon'ble Sir Henry Hardinge, G. C. B., one of Her Britannic Majesty's Hon'ble Privy Council, Governor-General, appointed by the Hon'ble Company to direct and control all their affairs in the East Indies, and by Maharajah Golab Singh in person.

ARTICLE 1.—The British Government transfers and makes over, for ever, in independent possession, to Maharajah Golab Singh, and the heirs male of his body, all the hilly or mountainous country, with its dependencies, situated on the eastward of the River Indus, and westward of the River Rávee, including Chumba and excluding Lahoul, being part of the territory ceded to the British Government by the Lahore State, according to the provisions of Article 4 of the Treaty of Lahore dated 9th March, 1846.

ARTICLE 2.—The eastern boundary of the tract, transferred by the foregoing article to Maharajah Golab Singh, shall be laid down by Commissioners appointed by the British Government and Maharajah Golab Singh respectively for that purpose, and shall be defined in a separate engagement after survey.

ARTICLE 3.—In consideration of the transfer made to him and his heirs by the provisions of the foregoing articles, Maharajah Golab Singh will pay to the British Government the sum of seventy-five lacs of rupees (Nánukshábee), fifty lacs to be paid on ratification of this treaty, and twenty-five lacs on or before the 1st of October of the current year A. D. 1846.

ARTICLE 4.—The limits of the territories of Maharajah Golab Singh shall not be at any time changed without the concurrence of the British Government.

ARTICLE 5.—Maharajah Golab Singh will refer to the arbitration of the British Government any disputes or questions that may arise between himself and the Government of Lahore, or any other neighbouring state, and will abide by the decision of the British Government.

ARTICLE 6.—Maharajah Golab Singh engages for himself and heirs to join, with the whole of his military force, the British troops, when employed within the hills, or in the territories adjoining his possessions.

ARTICLE 7.—Maharajah Golab Singh engages never to take, or retain, in his service any British subject, nor the subject of any European or American State, without the consent of the British Government.

Article 8.—Maharajah Golab Singh engages to respect, in regard to the territory transferred to him, the provisions of Articles 5, 6, and 7, of the separate engagement between the British Government, and the Lahore Durbar, dated 11th March, 1846.

Article 9.—The British Government will give its aid to Maharajah Golab Singh in protecting his territories from external enemies.

Article 10.—Maharajah Golab Singh acknowledges the supremacy of the British Government, and will, in token of such supremacy, present annually to the British Government one horse, twelve perfect shawl goats of approved breed (six male and six female), and three pairs of Kashmir shawls.

This Treaty, consisting of ten articles, has been this day settled by Frederick Currie, Esq., and Brevet-Major Henry Montgomery Lawrence, acting under the directions of the Right Hon'ble Sir Henry Hardinge, G. C. B., Governor-General, on the part of the British Government, and by Maharajah Golab Singh in person; and the said Treaty has been this day ratified by the seal of the Right Hon'ble Sir Henry Hardinge, G. C. B., Governor-General.

Done at Amritsar, this 16th day of March, in the year of our Lord 1846, corresponding with the 17th day of Rubbee-ool-awul, 1762, Hijree.

APPENDIX No. 2.

Kashmir Manufactures.

First and foremost among the manufactures of Kashmir must be placed this, its most costly as well as most renowned and beautiful. The most expensive variety of shawls are the *woven* (though the *hand worked* ones are generally the most admired by all but connoisseurs in this department); next the hand worked in, andon pushmeena; next the hand worked in silk on black linen with a pushmeena border; and cheapest of all the hand worked in silk on black linen with a silk fringe, though some of the last named kind are inferior in beauty to none. In this work are also made table covers and cushions, the most curious and striking being the *Rajah* pattern. It is impossible to give the rates of shawls, as their prices vary from Rs. 30 to thousands of rupees.

Shawl making.

In making jewellery the Kashmeris are very ingenious, and though their work has not that lightness so charming in that of Delhi, it has a peculiar style of its own which it were vain to imitate. In the plain gold they make every imaginable article of jewellery, charging at the rate of Rs. 2 a tolah for the material, and 2 annas in the rupee for workmanship; they sometimes introduce precious stones, principally *opals, carbuncles, bloodstones, agates,* and *turquoises;* all of these however

Gold Work.

Precious Stones.

it is best to avoid, unless the purchaser is a good judge; as at least three-fourths of those sold are clever imitations.

Silver Work.

The plain silver work is remarkable for its pure white colour, elegance of design, and beautiful carving; in it they make, *tea sets* and *trays*, *serais* or water bottles, *vases*, *ágdáns*, *bracelets*, *brooches*, *earrings*, and many other articles too numerous to mention. The principal patterns carved on it are the *shawl* pattern, and *double shawl* pattern; the latter being the more elaborate; the rates are from 2 to 4 annas in the rupee weight for workmanship, the material being paid for by its weight in rupees.

Gold and Silver Work.

This of all the manufactures seems most sought after by Europeans; it is extremely beautiful, and, except for articles that have much wear and tear on them, lasts well. The work consists principally *tea sets*, *trays*, *goblets*, *serais*, *claret jugs*, *drinking cups*, *bracelets*, *brooches*, *earrings*, *buttons*, &c.; but they can make any shape or form to order; the work is of silver, a design, generally the shawl pattern, being picked out in gold on it and afterwards embossed; the rates are 6 annas in the rupee, over and above its weight in silver.

Copper Work.

Their copper work is one of the most beautiful of their manufactures. It is composed of copper and tin, and the effect is exactly that of very old carved silver that has been buried for ages, and dug up again; this antique appearance constitutes its greatest charm, an article just made to order looking about a thousand years old. They work it up into *drinking vessels* and *goblets* of many different kinds, *tea* and *coffee sets, salvers, trays, vases, claret jugs*, &c.; in fact they can make any shape to order, and in this respect it will be found well to trust to their taste, as the Kashmiri has a correct eye, he never errs in form, and very seldon in color. This work is sold by weight, the rates being from 6 to 7 rupees the seer and the purchaser should insist on English weights.

Papier-mache.

The name given to this kind of work conveys no idea whatever of it, being so tolerably different to any thing sold under that name in Europe. The mode of making it is this:— The article is first fashioned in wood, then painted white and burnished with a smooth stone; after being thus prepared, the desired pattern is painted and illuminated on it, and finally varnished. It is extremly beautiful; among the patterns used are the *shawl, double shawl, black shawl*, and *white shawl*, the latter being very delicate and light looking; also the *Gulmarg*, the *vine*, the *rajah*, and *devil* pattern; the two last mamed are curious and fanciful, but the colors in them are rather crude. The articles made are principally *blotting cases, inkstands, card trays, candlesticks, toilet sets, boxes* of all kinds, and even *tables* and *chairs;* the effect however is not so happy in such large pieces, what was delicate and lovely in a small compass becoming dull and heavy in so large a body; if they enlarge their patterns to suit the size of the object the effect would be good, and probably there would be no difficulty in getting this done to order. Purchasers will be guided as to what they should pay by looking over their order books.

APPENDIX No. 3.

Treaty of Trade with Eastern Turkestan.

FOREIGN DEPARTMENT (POLITICAL);
Simla, the 24th June 1870.

No. 1070.—Some clerical errors having appeared in Notification dated 16th May 1870, No. 788P., the following revised Notification is published for general information:—

TREATY between the British Government and HIS HIGHNESS MAHARAJAH RUNBEER SINGH, G. C. S. I., *Maharajah of Jummoo and Kashmir, his heirs and successors, executed on the one part by* THOMAS DOUGLAS FORSYTH, C. B., *in virtue of the full powers vested in him by His Excellency the Right Hon'ble* RICHARD SOUTHWELL BOURKE, *Earl of Mayo, Viscount Mayo of Monycrower, Baron Naas of Naas,* K. P., G. M. S. I., P. C., &c., &c., &c., *Viceroy and Governor-General of India, and on the other part by* HIS HIGHNESS MAHARAJAH RUNBEER SINGH *aforesaid in person.*

Whereas, in the interest of the high contracting parties and their respective subjects, it is deemed desirable to afford greater facilities than at present exist for the development and security of trade with Eastern Turkestan, the following Articles have, with this object, been agreed upon:—

Article I.

With the consent of the Maharajah, officers of the British Government will be appointed to survey the trade-routes through the Maharajah's territories from the British frontier of Lahoul to the territories of the Ruler of Yarkund, including the route *viâ* the Chang Chemoo Valley. The Maharajah will depute an officer of his Government to accompany the surveyors, and will render them all the assistance in his power. A map of the routes surveyed will be made, an attested copy of which will be given to the Maharajah.

Article II.

Whichever route towards the Chang Chemoo Valley shall, after examination and survey as above, be declared by the British Government to be the best suited for the development of trade with Eastern Turkestan, shall be declared by the Maharajah to be a free highway in perpetuity and at all times for all travellers and traders.

Article III.

For the supervision and maintenance of the road in its entire length through the Maharajah's territories, the regulation of traffic on the free highway, described in

Article II, the enforcement of regulations that may be hereafter agreed upon, and the settlement of disputes between carriers, traders, travellers, or other using that road, in which either of the parties, or both of them, are subjects of the British Government or of any Foreign State, two Commissioners shall be annually appointed, one by the British Government, and the other by the Maharajah. In the discharge of their duties, and as regards the period of their residence, the Commissioners shall be guided by such rules as are now separately framed, and may from time to time hereafter be laid down by the joint authority of the British Government and the Maharajah.

Article IV.

The jurisdiction of the Commissioners shall be defined by a line on each side of the road at a maximum width of two Statute *kos*, except where it may be deemed by the Commissioners necessary to include a wider extent for grazing grounds. Within this maximum width the surveyors appointed under Article I shall demarcate and map the limits of jurisdiction which may be decided on by the Commissioners as most suitable, including grazing grounds, and the jurisdiction of the Commissioners shall not extend beyond the limits so demarcated. The land included within these limits shall remain in the Maharajah's independent possession, and subject to the stipulations contained in this Treaty. The Maharajah shall continue to possess the same rights of full sovereignty therein as in any other part of his territories, which rights shall not be interfered with in any way by the Joint Commissioners.

Article V.

The Maharajah agrees to give all possible assistance in enforcing the decisions of the Commissioners, and in preventing the breach or evasion of the regulations established under Article III.

Article VI.

The Maharajah agrees that any person, whether a subject of the British Government, or of the Maharajah, or of the Ruler of Yarkund, or of any Foreign State may settle at any place within the jurisdiction of the two Commissioners, and may provide, keep, mountain, and let for hire at different stages, the means of carriage and transport for the purposes of trade.

Article VII.

The two Commissioners shall be empowered to establish supply depôts, and to authorize other persons to establish supply depôts at such places on the road as may appear to them suitable; to fix the rates at which provisions shall be sold to traders, carriers, settlers, and others; and to fix the rent to be charged for the use of any rest-houses or serais that may be established on the road. The officers of the British Government in Kullu, &c., and the officers of the Maharajah in Ladakh, shall be instructed to use their best endeavours to supply provisions on the indent of the Commissioners at market rates.

Article VIII.

The Maharajah agrees to levy no transit duty whatever on the aforesaid free highway; and the Maharajah further agrees to abolish all transit duties levied within his territories on goods transmitted in bond, through His Highness's territories from Eastern Turkestan to India, and *vice versâ*, on which bulk may not be broken within the territories of His Highness. On goods imported into or exported from His Highness's territory, whether by the aforesaid free highway or any other route, the Maharajah may levy such import or export duties as he may think fit.

Article IX.

The British Government agree to levy no duty on goods transmitted in bond through British India to Eastern Turkestan, or to the territories of His Highness the Maharajah. The British Government further agree to abolish the export duties now levied on shawls and other textile fabrics manufactured in the territories of the Maharajah and exported to countries beyond the limits of British India.

Article X.

This Treaty, consisting of ten articles, has this day been concluded by Thomas Douglas Forsyth, C.B., in virtue of the full powers vested in him by His Excellency the Right

Hon'ble Richard Southwell Bourke, Earl of Mayo, Viscount Mayo of Monycrower, Baron Naas, of Naas, K.P., G.M.S.I., P. C., &c., &c., Viceroy and Governor-General of India, on the part of the British Government, and by His Highness Maharajah Runbeer Sing, aforesaid; and it is agreed that a copy of this Treaty, duly ratified by His Excellency the Viceroy and Governor-General of India, shall be delivered to the Maharajah on or before the 7th September 1870.

Signed, sealed and exchanged at Sealkote on the second day of April in the year of our Lord 1870, corresponding with the 22nd day of Bysakh Sumbut 1927.

This Treaty was ratified by His Excellency the Viceroy and Governor-General of India at Sealkote on the 2nd day of May in the year 1870.

The following rules, for the guidance of the Joint Commissioners appointed under Article III of the above Treaty, are published for general information:—

Rules for the guidance of the Joint Commissioners appointed for the new route to Eastern Turkestan.

I.—As it is impossible, owing to the character of the climate, to retain the Commissioners throughout the year, the period during which they shall exercise their authority shall be taken to commence on 15th May, and to end on 1st December, or till such further time as the passage of traders renders their residence on the road necessary.

II.—During the absence of either Commissioner, cases may be heard and decided by the other Commissioner, subject to appeal to the Joint Commissioners.

III.—In the months when the Joint Commissioners are absent, *i. e.*, between 1st December and 15th May, or the dates that may hereafter be determined, all cases which may arise shall be decided by the Wuzeer of Ladakh, subject to appeal to the Joint Commissioners.

IV.—The Joint Commissioners shall not interfere in cases other than those which affect the development, freedom, and safety of the trade, and the objects for which the treaty is concluded, and in which one of the parties or both are either British subjects, or subjects of a foreign State.

V.—In civil disputes the Commissioners shall have power to dispose of all cases, whatever be the value of the property in litigation.

VI.—When the Commissioners agree, their decision shall be final in all cases. When they are unable to agree, the parties shall have the right of nominating a single arbitrator, and shall bind themselves in writing to abide by his award. Should the parties not be able to agree upon a single arbitrator, each party shall name one, and the two Commissioners shall name a third, and the decision of the majority of the arbitrators shall be final.

VII.—In criminal cases of the kind referred to in clause 4, the powers of the Commissioners shall be limited to offences such as in British territory would be tried by a subordinate Magistrate of the first class, and as far as possible the procedure of the Criminal Procedure Code shall be followed. Cases of a more heinous kind and of offences against the special laws regarding religion in Kashmir should be made over to the Maharajah for trial if the accused be not an European British subject: in the latter case he should be forwarded to the nearest British Court of competent jurisdiction for trial.

VIII.—All fines levied in criminal cases, and all stamp receipts levied according to the rates in force for civil suits in the Maharajah's dominions, shall be credited to the Kashmir Treasury. Persons sentenced to imprisonment shall, if British subjects, be sent to the nearest British Jail. If not British subjects, the offenders shall be made over for imprisonment in the Maharajah's jails.

IX.—If any places come within the line of road from which the towns of Lehee are supplied with fuel or wood for building purposes, the Joint Commissioners shall so arrange with the Wuzeer of Ladakh that those supplies are not interfered with.

X.—Whatever transactions take place within the limits of the road shall be considered to refer to goods in bond. If a trader opens his load, and disposes of a portion, he shall not be subject to any duty, so long as the goods are not taken for consumption into the Maharajah's territory across the line of road. And goods left for any length of time in the line of road subject to the jurisdiction of the Commissioners, shall be free.

XI.—Where a village lies within the jurisdiction of the Joint Commissioners, then as regards the collection of revenue, or in any case, where there is necessity for the interference of the usual revenue authorities in matters having no connection with trade, the Joint Commissioners have no power whatever to interfere; but to prevent misunderstanding, it is advisable that the revenue officials should first communicate with the Joint Commissioners before proceeding to take action against any person within their jurisdiction. The Joint Commissioners can then exercise their discretion to deliver up the person sought, or to make a summary inquiry to ascertain whether their interference is necessary or not.

XII.—The Maharajah agrees to give Rs. 5,000 this year for the construction of the road and bridges; and in future years His Highness agrees to give Rs. 2,000 per annum for the maintenance of the road and bridges. Similarly for the repairs of serais, a sum of Rs. 100 per annum for each serai will be given. Should further expenditure be necessary, the Joint Commissioners will submit a special report to the Maharajah, and ask for a specific grant. This money will be expended by the Joint Commissioners, who will employ free labor at market rates for this purpose. The officers in Ladakh and in British territory shall be instructed to use their best endeavours to supply laborers on the indent of the Commissioners at market rates. No tolls shall be levied on the bridges on this line of road.

XIII.—As a temporary arrangement, and until the line of road has been demarcated, or until the end of this year, the Joint Commissioners shall exercise the powers described in these rules over the several roads taken by the traders through Ladakh from Lahoul and Spiti.

APPENDIX No. 4.

The following TABLES OF TRADE between the Kashmir and the Jummoo territories and the Panjab are extracted from the "*Report of the Trade and Resources of the Countries on the North-Western boundary of British India,*" published by the Panjab Government in 1862,—the latest source of information upon this subject:—

EXPORTS TO THE PANJAB.

No.	Names of Articles.	From		Total.
		Kashmir.	Jummoo.	
1	Pushmeena—Shawl Fabrics ...	12,00,000	60,000	12,60,000
2	Woollen Cloths and Blankets ...	40,000	20,000	60,000
3	Chob-i-koot, an indigenous wood ...	16,500	....	16,500
4	Saffron ...	20,000	....	20,000
5	Quince Seed ...	5,000	2,000	7,000
6	Fruits—Apples, Pears, Walnuts ...	15,000	15,000	30,000
7	Raw Silk ...	7,000	....	7,000
8	Paper, Kashmiree ...	15,000	....	15,000
9	Timber—Deodár ...	....	3,00,000	3,00,000
10	Papier-maché ...	6,000	....	6,000
11	Chirkee Wood ...	....	5,000	5,000
	Grocery, Spices, Medicines, &c.			
12	Cummin Seed ...	3,000	....	3,000
13	Other Spices, Drugs, &c. ...	26,000	74,000	1,00,000
14	Grain, Til, Rice ...	....	20,000	20,000
15	Ghee ...	....	1,50,000	1,50,000
	Total Exports, Rs. ...	13,53,500	6,46,000	19,99,500

IMPORTS FROM THE PANJAB.

No.	Names of Articles.	To Kashmir.	To Jummoo.	Total.
1	English Piece-goods, Cotton, Silken, Woollen, &c.	75,000	3,36,000	4,11,000
2	Country Cloths, Cotton, Silken, Brocades of Benares, &c.	40,000	1,24,000	1,64,000
3	Cotton ...	10,000	15,000	25,000
4	Blankets, Woollen, Felts, &c. ...	....	25,000	25,000
5	Kulabutoon, gold and silver thread, lace, &c.	5,000	15,000	20,000
6	Jewels, silver, gold, precious stones, &c.	....	75,000	75,000
7	Tea ...	25,000	5,000	30,000
8	Salt, Panjab rock salt ...	2,00,000	3,50,000	5,50,000
9	Sugar ...	28,000	40,000	68,000
10	Coarse Sugar and Molasses ...	2,000	40,000	42,000
11	Indigo ...	3,000	5,000	8,000
12	Lac, a dye ...	10,000	2,000	12,000
13	Other Dyes, Spices, Drugs, Spirits, &c.	50,000	80,000	1,30,000
14	Haberdashery, Leathers, Furs, Mats, Persian Reeds, &c.	15,000	25,000	40,000
15	Porcelain ...	4,000	1,000	5,000
16	Copper and Tin ...	30,000	45,000	75,000
17	Utensils (Brass, &c.) ...	6,000	10,000	16,000
18	Fruits, Afghanistan ...	7,000	10,000	17,000
19	Snuff, Peshawur ...	5,000	1,000	6,000
20	Grain ...	4,000	46,000	50,000
21	Horses, Afghanistan and Panjab ...	....	20,000	20,000
22	Other Cattle ...	....	10,000	10,000
	Total Imports, Rs. ...	5,29,000	13,20,300	18,49,000

APPENDIX No. 5.

*Game in Kashmir and adjoining countries.**

The best months for shooting about Kashmir are from the middle of April to the middle of July, and from the middle of September to November. During the intervening months rain falls frequently and heavily upon the mountains; the jungle is rank, high, and malarious, and the *ibex* and *markhor* grounds are often covered with immense flocks of sheep and goats, and droves of ponies and cattle, which are annually sent up from the plains to graze. *Barasing* are not usually met with until the middle of September, although they may occasionally be found in the middle of August, and with fully developed horns. After November the hunting grounds usually become inaccessible from frost and snow. The sportman should provide himself with Montgomerie's *Jummoo and Kashmir Map*, and his *Kashmir Route Map*, procurable from the publishers of this work.

Barasing or *hungul* is found in Loláb, Lár, the Sind Valley, Gurais, Tilail, Dachinpára, Wardwan, and throughout the mountain range extending from the Takhti-Súlimán towards the Wardwan and Kishtwár.

Bears are found in all parts of Kashmir, particularly in Loláb and the Nowboog valley; and although far less numerous than formerly, they are still very common. The *brown* or *red* variety generally resides high up, while the *black* is

* The author is indebted to the late Lieutenant-Colonel H. C. Cuppage, B.S.C., for much information upon this subject. He was well known as one of the keenest sportsmen in India.

usually found lower down; they are both chiefly herbivorous, but also partly carnivorous; they lose their long fur in July, and during the rainy season their skins are not easily preserved, as they do not dry, and the hair readily falls off. During the fruit season, the black bear is very obnoxious to the villagers residing near the hills, and its ravages in the gardens and cornfields, which it usually visits shortly after sunset, are often very considerable.

Burrul is chiefly found in the vicinity of the Pangong Lake and the Karakoorum mountains to the north-east of Kashmir.

Dogs.—The *wild dog* is gregarious, and large packs often infest Lár, Dachinpára, the Wardwan, Drás, and Ladák; they sometimes commit great havoc amongst the sheep and cattle grazing upon the mountain downs or *margs* of those districts; and when pressed by hunger, they will, it is said, destroy children, and even men and women.

Fox and Jackal are common in Kashmir, and some fair hunting was obtained with a small pack of hounds belonging to the 7th Hussars, during the season of 1865. A *black fox* is found in the Karakoorum, and also a large species of *hyæna*, the *lynx*, and *wolves*; the *flying-fox* abounds in Gurais in the early part of the season, where it is shot at night with the aid of lighted torches.

Gooral is found in the Pir Panjál, in Dráwur, and Kishtwár.

Ibex is found in Dráwar-trans-Kishanganga, probably on the northern side of Loláb, in Lár, the Sind Valley,

Gurais, Tilail, Astor, Drás, Ladák, Dachinpára, and the Wardwan. The *Tibetan ibex* is small, of a dark slate or almost black colour, and its horns are thinner and more wrinkled than those of the common variety.

KHAKAR or the *barking deer* is usually found only upon the southern and western slopes of the Fati and Pir Panjáls.

LEOPARDS are found all round the Kashmir Valley, and also in márkhor ground, but they chiefly infest the grazing grounds or *margs*, where they sometimes commit great havoc amongst the sheep and cattle. The *ounce, snow or white leopard*, has been seen in Tilail.

MARKHOR.—This animal, like the *barasing* and *ibex*, is migratory; it is found all over the Pir Panjál beyond the Barramgalla pass, upon the mountains between the Jhelam and Kishanganga Rivers, including Gurais, Tilail, and Astor, and probably also upon those lying south of Kashmir. The horns of the márkhor of the Nanga Parbat or *Deermeer*, in Astor, have only one curve; they are massive and are said sometimes to attain a length of sixty inches; the animal is very rarely met with by the European sportsman, but an illustration of its horns may be seen in "Cunningham's Ladák."

MUSK DEER is found in all parts of Kashmir at a certain elevation, and prticularly in Lár, and along the Sind Valley.

OVIS POLII is a species of sheep inhabiting Chittrál and the neighbouring countries, which, however, are inaccessible to the European sportsman, by whom only its horns have as yet been discovered.

SHAPOO, the *ooreál* or *ovis Vignii*, and the TIBETAN ANTELOPE, called *goa* and *tchiroo*, are found in Ladák, Pangong, Chángchenmo, and the Karakoorum.

SURROW is found upon the Panjáls, in Dachinpára, the Sind Valley, and probably also on the mountains to the north-west of Kashmir.

THAR is found upon the Panjáls, in Banihál, the southern portion of Wardwan and Kishtwár.

WILD HORSE or ASS called *kiung*, the OVIS AMMON, and the YAK, are found in the same localities as the shápoo and the Tibetan antelope.

Many kinds of game-birds are also found in Kashmir and the neighbouring provinces, and the following are some of them :—

GROUSE.—The *snow* variety is found in the vicinity of the Pángong lake, and also the Tsomonáng la jhe, a lake situated to the south of Rudokh, and discovered in 1865 by J. Low, Esq., of the Indian Survey Department, by whom it is supposed to communicate with the Pángong.

PARTRIDGE, of which the *black*, *chikore*, *grey*, and *snow* species are met with in many parts.

PHEASANT.—The varieties met with are the *argus*, *moonál*, *kullich*, *koklas*, and the *snow*.

PLOVER.—The *golden* variety is found near Golábbágh in Ladák.

QUAIL.—The common kind, and the jack *snipe;* the latter is found in Ladák, and probably in other places.

WATERFOWL, *geese, ducks, teal,* and many other kinds are met with in great abundance during the cold months, espicially upon the Woolar Lake in the Kashmir Valley.

WOODCOCK is also found in and around Kashmir.

APPENDIX No. 6.

Rules for Visitors.

PUNJAB GOVERNMENT NOTIFICATION,
FOREIGN DEPARTMENT.
The 29th March 1875.

No. 557.—Notification—The following Rules for the guidance of travellers visiting the dominions of His Highness the Maharajah of Jamoo and Kashmir, having received the sanction of His Excellency the Governor-General in Council, are published for general information:—

1. The Punjab Government no longer issues passes for visitors to Kashmir.

The number of Military Officers in Kashmir *at one time* is restricted to two hundred. The disposal of passes for this number, less a certain number reserved for the Punjab Frontier Force, is with His Excellency the Commander-in-Chief. Frontier Force Officers, desiring to visit Kashmir, must apply to the Brigadier-General Commanding. Civilians and Military Officers in Civil employ, but a small proportion of whom under the leave rules can visit Kashmir the same season, do not require any passes, but they should report their intention to travel in Kashmir to the Assistant Secretary, Lahore, and can obtain at the Secretariat Office, Lahore, a copy of the Rules to which they must conform.

2. There are four authorized routes for European visitors to Kashmir:—

First.—The principal road from the plains by Bhimber and Rajaori. This road over the Pir Panjál Range is not open till May, and is closed by the snow at the beginning of November; it is the old imperial road.

No.	Name of Stage.	Distance in kos.
1	Bhimber	
2	Serai Saidabád	8
3	Naushera	7
4	Serai Changas	7
5	Rojaori (Rámpúr)	8
6	Thána Mandi	8
7	Báramgalla	7
8	Poshiána	6
9	Serai Aliabad...	7
10	Dubjián (Hirpur)	6
11	Shapiyon	6
12	Ramú	7
13	Srinagar	9
		86

At all these stages the Maharajah has had rest houses erected.

[NOTE.—In calculating distances the kos may be taken as equivalent to about 1½ English miles.]

At the Bhimber dâk bungalow a Khansámá, with the usual staff of servants, is kept up for the convenience of travellers. At all the stages between Serai Saidabad and Thána Mandi, both inclusive, ordinary Europe liquors and stores are procurable.

From the 25th March a hill cart service will be maintained during the season by the dâk bungalow khansámá at Gujrát, between that station and Bhimber. Fare, Rs. 11 per seat.

Second.—The road from the plains of Kattipanch, Uri, and Báramula. This road is open in April, but it is difficult and is not recommended.

Third.—The road from Murree by Chikár and Báramula :—

No.	Name of Stage.	Distance in miles.
1	Murree	......
2	Dewal	12
3	Kohála	10
4	Chikár	11
5	Rhára	9
6	Thandáli	14
7	Gharri	8
8	Hattián	12
9	Chakoli	14
10	Uri	14
11	Urambú*	10
12	Báramula	13
13	Srinagar	......

* *Rampore*, about a mile and half further on, is now the halting place, Urambú having been abandoned.—J. I.

There are dâk bungalows at all the stages. The road generally is good and travelling easy. The stages from Rhára to Thandáli, and from Hattián to Chakoti, are troublesome, and in coming from Gharri to Hattián there is a mountain stream to cross, which may cause considerable delay when it is swollen by the rains. The last stage, from Báramula to Srinagar is usually done by boat in two days, the first night being spent at Sopar. The old road from Kohála to Hattián, *via* Damia and Chikár, is closed to travellers.

Fourth.—The road from Peshawar through Hazára and by Muzaffarabád, Katlai and Báramula. This road is comparatively easy and is open throughout the year.

The special permission of the Panjáb Government must be obtained by travellers proposing to travel from Kashmir to Simla (*or vice versâ*) across the Hills, or to the plains, (*or vice versâ*) by Kishtwár, Bhadrawár and Chamba. British Officers are prohibited from making application on behalf of themselves or their friends direct to His Highness the Maharajah or his officers, for permission to proceed to or from Kashmir by any but the authorized routes.

(*Note.*—Throughout Chamba territory rest houses and supplies for travellers will be found.)

All other routes are positively forbidden.

3.—Carriage and Coolies.

The rates ordinarily payable per stage are :—

Per cooly	...	...	... 4 annas.
„ kahar	...	...	... 6 „
„ pony or mule ...		...	... 8 „

Where the rates according to schedules attested by the district officer are higher than the above, payment sha be made at such higher rates.

A cooly's load shall not exceed 25 seers, nor that of a pony or mule exceed 2 maunds. Travellers are particularly required to be careful that their servants do not overload coolies or cattle. A pair of scales will be kept at each stage, and when objection is taken to the weight of a load travellers are bound to comply with a request that such load should be weighed.

Coolies must be paid daily, and travellers should see payment made in their own presence.

4.—Travellers on reaching a stage must send forward to the next stage notice of their requirements, otherwise delay will be experienced.

5.—In returning from Kashmir coolies or carriage are not to be taken beyond the Maharajah's frontier, or the first stage beyond the frontier.

6.—Unless travellers encamp at the fixed stages and encamping grounds, there is no certainty that supplies will be available. They should not encamp within villages.

7.—Arrangements for coolies and carriage are made as follows:—

(A.) On the Murree road by a contractor who has the line of road from Báramula to Kohála, and is bound to keep 30 mules or ponies and 20 coolies at each stage. He has 2 sepoys and the village shop-keeper at each stage as his agents, and application for carriage should be made to them or to the Thánadár.

(B.) On the Muzaffarabad road the same contractor as on the Murree road will supply carriage on due notice being given beforehand. In case of need travellers may apply to the officials of the Rajahs of Kathai and Uri within their respective territories, elsewhere to the lambadárs.

(C.) On the Bhimber road carriage is supplied by contractors who are bound to keep up at each stage 15 mules or ponies and 15 coolies.

(D.) At Srinagar, the Bábu deputed to attend on European visitors supplies carriage, &c., 24 hours' previous notice is requisite.

From Rámu to Pir Panjál carriage is supplied by one contractor; from Thána to Bhimber by another. Both these have as agents the village shop-keepers along the road. From Thána to Báramgalla the subjects of the Maharajah serve as coolies; from Báramgalla to Shapiyan those of Rajah Moti Singh of Punch; from Shapiyan to Báramgalla those of the Maharajah. The Thánadár of Báramgalla is responsible for the coolies coming from Rajah Moti Singh's territories; he will also see to the supply of coolies along the Punch road, having as agents the lambadárs of the villages.

Travellers must make their own arrangements with the contractors. They are recommended to use mules or ponies wherever possible rather than coolies.

8. A book in the form annexed will be presented at each stage, in which every traveller is required to write legibly his name, rank and station, the date of his arrival and departure, and the amount of carriage taken by him.

Name, rank and station of Visitor.	Date and hour of arrival.	Date and hour of departure.	Stage to which proceeding.	Amount of carriage taken.		Remarks.
				Coolies.	Mules or ponies.	

9. When going on shooting excursions, visitors must take carriage and supplies with them, and are not to demand them in places where no provision is made for

supplying them. They are not to press into their service the people of the country as beaters for game.

10. Travellers must not interfere with any Kashmir officials, and no calls are to be made on them except in real emergencies. All payments are to be made at the rates demanded, which, if exorbitant, can be reported to the officer on duty at Srinagar.

11. Should travellers have reason to consider that they, or their servants, have been ill-treated or affronted, they are strictly forbidden to adopt any other means of obtaining redress than by making complaint to the officials of the Maharajah on the spot, and immediately reporting the circumstances to the British officer on duty at Srinagar. At Srinagar complaints are to be preferred direct to the officer on duty; and are not to be preferred in any Kashmir Court.

12. Visitors are forbidden to take away with them from Kashmir, on any pretext whatever, any subjects of the Maharajah without obtaining permission, and a pass port from the Kashmir Authorities.

13. Travellers are strictly required to settle all accounts before they leave Kashmir, and are responsible that the debts of their servants are similarly discharged. Should any officer of Government leave Kashmir without discharging his debts, he will not be permitted ever to re-visit it.

14. Visitors are prohibited from receiving any presents whatever during their stay from the Kashmir durbar or officials.

15. Visitors are required to take care that the Customs Regulations of His Highness the Maharajah are in no way violated by themselves or their servants.

16. Officers invited by His Highness the Maharajah to evening entertainments at the palace are required to appear in ordinary evening dress or uniform. By order of the Hon'ble the Lieutenant-Governor.

(Sd.) T. H. THORNTON,
Secretary to Government, Punjab.

APPENDIX No. 7.

Kashmir Postal Rules.

PANJAB GAZETTE.

No. 673, GENERAL DEPARTMENT,

16*th March*, 1867.

The following arrangements for postal communication with Kashmir during the ensuing season have been made in communication with the Kashmir Government and the Post-Master-General of the Panjab :—

I.—All letters for Srinagar and the Valley of Kashmir will be forwarded *viâ* Murree.

II.—At Murree the letters will be placed in a sealed bag and made over to an official of the Maharajah of Kashmir, who will convey the bag to the civil officer on duty at Srinagar.

III.—The bag will be opened and the letters sorted by an official attached to the office of the civil officer.

IV.—All letters for visitors at Srinagar and their followers will be distributed through the agency placed at the disposal of the civil officer. Other letters will be made over to the diwan of the Maharajah at Srinagar for distribution.

V.—In addition to the English postage, a fee equal to half the English postage will be levied on all letters delivered at Srinagar.

VI.—A post office will be opened at or near the residence of the civil officer for the convenience of visitors to Kashmir and their followers, and letters for British territory will be despatched in a sealed bag to Murree, and made over to the postal authorities at that place.

VII.—All covers intended for despatch from Srinagar to British territory by the above dâk—which for convenience will be designated the "Resident's dâk"—should be marked "Per Resident's dâk" in English, and signed at the lower left hand corner by the sender; they must further bear, in addition to the English postage, a Kashmir postage stamp of half the value of the English stamp required, otherwise they will be made over to the diwan to be returned to the sender, if known, or otherwise disposed of according to the rules of the Kashmir Post Office.

By order, &c.,

T. H. THORNTON,

Secretary to Government, Panjab.